AF879438

***WALL STREET JOURNAL* BEST-SELLING AUTHOR**

Beau Henderson, RICP®

NATIONAL SOCIAL SECURITY ADVISOR (NSSA®)

Social Security Clarity.

The Step-by-Step Path to Optimizing Your Retirement Benefits

UPDATED TO INCLUDE THE SOCIAL SECURITY FAIRNESS ACT

2025 EDITION

FOREWORD BY MARC KINER FOUNDER OF NSSA®

ISBN: 978-1-7347032-3-8

CONTENTS

STAY UPDATED ON SOCIAL SECURITY CHANGES

Our team is committed to providing you with reliable information and practical advice for optimizing your retirement journey. To stay up to date:

- **Sign up for free future PDF updates** to this book by visiting SocialSecurityClarity.com/resources. You will receive an email with each new edition to keep up-to-date with the latest changes impacting your Social Security benefits.
- **Subscribe to our YouTube Channel @richlifeadvisors** for additional insights and tips on navigating Social Security decisions and retirement income planning.

FOREWORD

Social Security and a sense of humor. This combination does not come about very often. Beau Henderson's book on Social Security combines humor with a frank discussion on Social Security. The Social Security Act was signed into law on August 14, 1935, and today provides benefits to 67 million folks nationwide. In 2023, Social Security Administration paid $1.3 trillion to beneficiaries. Social Security is a very large government program, and many people believe that Social Security is also very complicated. However, Beau breaks down the Social Security rules in easy-to-understand terms and combines a unique sense of humor to keep the reader engaged and asking for more.

Regardless, if you are single, married, have young children, a surviving spouse, divorced or a public employee, this Social Security guide will help you to understand your Social Security claiming strategies resulting in larger benefits over your lifetime and over the lifetime of a surviving spouse (if applicable).

Beau is a Lifetime member of the National Social Security Advisor Certificate program. This certificate denotes advanced education in Social Security and related claiming strategies. Earning the National Social Security Advisor Certificate, Beau has taken an in-depth class on Social Security and passed an assessment. Beau has joined a limited number of advisors that have earned this certificate nationwide.

You have taken the first step in understanding and maximizing your Social Security benefits by reading this guide on Social Security. Beau will help you to understand your benefits and the options that are available resulting in the maximum amount of Social Security benefits to be received over your lifetime.

Marc Kiner,
NSSA®,
National Social Security Advisor Certificate Holder,
Creator of the National Social Security Advisor Certificate program

INTRODUCTION

In retirement planning, the Social Security claiming decision affects everyone that has paid into the benefit and who lives to full retirement age. For most households it's the largest income source in retirement, yet it's often brushed over, neglected, or worse—mishandled by the ones we turn to for advice.

There is no cookie cutter answer for how to take this benefit as each household's circumstances vary widely. With unique timelines, income gaps, assets, and other variables at play, informed decision-making is crucial. Sadly, only a very small percentage of people get as much from the benefit as possible. This book was written to change that. My ultimate goal is to equip readers with the knowledge to confidently navigate Social Security decisions, helping ensure they maximize their hard-earned benefits.

Historically speaking, if you can find a better way to do something, chances are good you'll make some serious cash.

Henry Ford invented neither the automobile nor the assembly line, but he found a better way to maximize the efficiency of both, and his inflation-adjusted net worth upon death was a reported $188.1 billion.

The founder and builder of the McDonald's Corp., Ray Kroc, found a better way to levy quality checks on the mass production of fast food and went to amass a $500 million fortune, even though at the age of 52, he was just a milkshake machine salesman.

As a retirement professional, I've talked to thousands of people who are preparing to file or have already filed their Social Security. They come to my Social Security workshops with their questions because they've heard things and read things and they are also wondering, "What if there is a better way to claim my Social Security benefit than I currently know?"

- A better way to file that will give you the most dollars?
- A better way to strategize and take care of your spouse?
- A better way to increase your income by potentially lowering your taxes?
- A better way to help your income last as long as you do?

I'm here to tell you that yes, there is a better way!

While 53.7 million retired workers and their dependents receive Social Security benefits per month, of that number, fewer than 2.2 million people have elected to receive the maximum amount of benefits allowed by law.[1] US households are leaving approximately $3.4 trillion on the table[2] when it comes to this benefit because they aren't making the best decision in most cases. Income needs are growing while traditional sources of retirement funds are shrinking.

When you have better information, you can make a better decision. When you have good information and know the rules that apply to your household, you can take advantage of the options and strategies that can result in tens of thousands to hundreds of thousands dollars of additional lifetime income. Most households don't do better with this decision simply because *they don't know better*. There is a knowledge gap.

---

1 *Social Security Administration Fact Sheet April 2024 https://www.ssa.gov/news/press/factsheets/basicfact-alt.pdf*

2 *United Income: "The Retirement Solution Hiding in Plain Sight: How Much Retirees Would Gain by Improving Social Security Decisions" 2019*

Not only is there a better way, but my goal in writing this book is to help you know the rules that apply to your household and be equipped to make suitable decisions.

MY PROMISE TO YOU

Eight years into my career as a financial advisor, I had an eye-opening lunch meeting with a mentor of mine (who for the purposes of this book, we'll call Thomas). Thomas, a smart and successful businessman who I know loved his family, was upset that he made a mistake when he filed for his Social Security benefit. He filed for his Social Security at his full retirement age because he was advised that he could and should take his income at full retirement age as there is no longer an earnings cap. The problem is the person that gave him the advice was leaving out a lot of context from Thomas' household.

Thomas worked earning significant income until his early 70's, his wife was several years younger, and he was already dealing with some genetic heart issues that left men in his family with shorter than average life expectancies. Statistically his wife will outlive him 10 or more years, equating to over $200,000 of unclaimed lifetime benefits that their household was entitled to. On my way home from that meeting, I realized the gravity of the situation. If someone as smart and successful as Thomas could make these mistakes, how many others were in the same position?

That was the day I realized that I was doing a major disservice to the people I worked with if I couldn't help them figure out how to be better equipped to make a good decision when claiming their Social Security benefits.

In the financial services industry, the majority of professionals do not address Social Security claiming optimization with their clients. There are two problems I see that come up most often:

1. They do not know how to help with the Social Security decision because they are not taught, or don't seek this education and training to know the rules and know how to help.
2. They are not paid to give Social Security advice and could potentially have financial incentive to encourage you to take the benefit earlier in the timeline.

If you're here reading these words, it's because you're thinking about filing for Social Security and you're looking for your better way. If you've already filed, you might be wondering if you did the right thing. It may not be too late to change your mind and there may be options to claim additional money.

My promise to you as you read this book is simple: I aim to present the information you need to get the most out of your Social Security benefit. I'll show you:

- What questions to ask
- What questions may not apply to you and
- What mistakes to avoid

The master checklist that you will complete by going through this book or downloading a PDF at SocialSecurityClarity.com/resources is so comprehensive, you might even want to take it with you to your next meeting with your financial advisor. My goal is to help know the rules that apply to your household and be equipped to make a better decision and get as much money from your Social Security benefit as possible.

OUR ROADMAP

In part 1 of this book, we will explore how so many Americans get it wrong with the 5 biggest Social Security claiming mistakes to avoid. From there, part 2 will provide the path forward with a simple three-step process for making the right selection for your household. I encourage you to choose your own adventure and read only the chapters that may apply to your household to get the most out of this book for you.

You've worked hard for this benefit; you deserve to get the most out of it. Here's to finding your better way.

—Beau Henderson,
National Social Security Advisor (NSSA®),
Retirement Income Certified Professional (RICP®),
Behavioral Financial Advisor (BFA),
Certified Financial Fiduciary® (CFF)

WHAT'S NEW AT A GLANCE 2025

Social Security is likely to be one of, if not *the* largest, source of income in your retirement. This book has been designed to simplify the complex and ever-changing rules, providing you with a clear process to maximize your benefits and feel confident in your claiming decisions.

In 2025, even seemingly minor adjustments can have significant implications for retirement planning. Here's a summary of the key changes:

- **Cost-of-Living Adjustment (COLA):** Social Security recipients received a **2.5%** cost-of-living adjustment. Though seemingly routine, this adjustment is a unique attribute of this income source to help offset inflation.
- **Maximum Taxable Earnings:** This is the highest amount of income subject to Social Security taxes, currently set at **$176,100**. It's important for retirees because it determines how much they'll pay in Social Security taxes and influences the calculation of their benefits. Understanding this limit helps you plan your retirement finances accurately.
- **Earnings Test Thresholds:** The thresholds for the "earnings test" have been adjusted to **$23,400 (or $1,950 monthly).** These adjustments can affect retirees' decisions on employment and the timing of claiming Social Security benefits.

- **Earnings Limit at Full Retirement Age (FRA):** For individuals reaching full retirement age (FRA) in 2025, the earnings limit is **$62,160 (or $5,180 monthly).** This limit influences retirees' decisions on continuing to work and the timing of claiming benefits.
- While navigating these annual adjustments, it's also important to consider broader legislative changes that impact retirement planning. This book has been updated to reflect the implications of both **The SECURE Act** (2019) and **The SECURE Act 2.0** (2022). These Acts have significantly altered tax planning considerations for retirees by increasing the Required Minimum Distribution (RMD) age to 72 and then to 73, respectively. Additionally, starting January 1, 2033, the RMD age is scheduled to further increase to 75, impacting those born in 1960 or later.
- **Social Security Fairness Act (Signed into law on January 5, 2025):** In a landmark change, the Social Security Fairness Act eliminated both the Windfall Elimination Provision (WEP) and Government Pension Offset (GPO), benefiting nearly 3 million public sector retirees. This historic legislation means public servants like teachers, firefighters, and police officers no longer face reductions in their Social Security benefits due to their government pensions.

While these changes offer retirees a longer window to delay withdrawals from their retirement accounts, Chapter 2 delves into the nuanced tax-saving strategies amidst these shifts. Understanding these legislative changes is vital for optimizing retirement income and tax planning effectively.

Our team is committed to providing you with reliable information and practical advice for optimizing your retirement journey. To stay up to date:

- **Sign up for free future PDF updates** to this book by visiting SocialSecurityClarity.com/resources. You will receive an email with each new edition to keep up-to-date with the latest changes impacting your Social Security benefits.

- **Subscribe to our YouTube Channel @richlifeadvisors** for additional insights and tips on navigating Social Security decisions and retirement income planning.

PART 1

HOW PEOPLE GET IT WRONG—5 MAJOR MISTAKES

"It's good to learn from your mistakes. It's better to learn from other people's mistakes."
—WARREN BUFFETT

In Part 1 of this book, we delve into the critical importance of understanding and avoiding the most common pitfalls when navigating the complexities of Social Security, and what to do if you already chose the wrong strategy. Use this quick guide to determine which may be applicable to your scenario:

1. **Failing to coordinate your benefits**
   Must read for everyone

2. **Paying more than your share of taxes**
   Must read for everyone

3. **Robbing your spouse**
   Must read if you are married

4. **Shooting yourself in the foot while working like a dog**
   Must read if you plan to have earned wages when claiming retirement benefits

5. **Picking the wrong claiming strategy (and how to correct it)**
   Must read if you:
   - *Are entitled to a survivor's benefit in addition to your own benefit.*
   - *Are entitled to both a spousal benefit and a disability benefit.*
   - *Are receiving a spousal benefit because you are caring for a child who is under the age of 16.*
   - *Are receiving a spousal benefit because you are caring for a child who is disabled.*

CHAPTER 1

FAILING TO COORDINATE YOUR BENEFITS

As I shared in the introduction of this book, I had an eye-opening lunch meeting with a mentor of mine (who for the purposes of this book, we'll call Thomas). Thomas, a smart and successful businessman who I know loved his family, was upset that he made a mistake when he filed for his Social Security benefit. He filed for his Social Security at his full retirement age because he was advised that he could and should take his income at full retirement age as there is no longer an earnings cap. The problem is the person that gave him the advice was leaving out a lot of context from Thomas' household. Thomas worked earning significant income until his early 70's, his wife was several years younger, and he was already dealing with some genetic heart issues that left men in his family with shorter than average life expectancies. Statistically his wife will outlive him 10 or more years, equating to potentially over $200,000 of unclaimed lifetime benefits that their household was entitled to. This example underscores the importance that your Social Security claiming decision cannot happen in a vacuum and needs to be coordinated as part of a complete plan. (Want to know your household's potential unclaimed benefits? Visit SocialSecurityClarity.com/analyze).

Over the last decade I've talked to literally thousands of people during my Social Security optimization workshops, and in every venue, most of the households in the room have the opportunity to receive more from their Social Security benefit. Education and awareness of the rules that apply to your specific situation are the keys to closing the knowledge gap and equipping people to make better decisions and receive more money from their benefits.

Could that person be you?

Chances are, if you are reading this book, then you are already ahead of most people. Many Americans today are filing early without really considering all of the variables that determine if that is a good decision. Not only are they failing to increase the efficiency of their portfolio, but they are reducing the effectiveness of this lifetime benefit by not spending time to find their better way. This lack of planning can result in leaving tens of thousands to hundreds of thousands of dollars on the table. Many neglect to consider these unique considerations of Social Security as a retirement income source:

- Social Security gives you two very important benefits that your IRA, 401(k) and even your pension may not give you. It provides you with guaranteed income and regular cost-of-living adjustments that help you keep up with inflation.
- Social Security is a lifetime benefit, so the longer you live, the more total income dollars you will receive.
- There's a good statistical chance you will live longer than you think and have to retire earlier than planned.
- Because most companies are no longer holding your income money in pension plans, most people retire with most (if not all) of their retirement money accumulated in pre-tax investment accounts. This can expose you to market loss. The income you receive from Social Security is not exposed to market risk.
- The longer you wait to claim your Social Security benefit after reaching your Full Retirement Age (FRA), the more your benefit can grow. Your benefit will increase by 8% annually for each year you wait, up to age 70, without exposure to market risk.

- If you file early, a benefit reduction is locked in for life. It becomes the base from which all your future cost-of-living adjustments are made. Your benefit will increase with COLAs, but the reduction due to early filing will remain permanent.
- The break-even point is not a good rule of thumb when determining when to file because there are so many variables you have to take into consideration when filing, such as inflation, taxes and the cost-of-living increases. It is also overly simplistic for most retirees as it does not typically account for survivor benefits or spousal implications, which can be critical for married couples.
- The difference between the worst way and the best way to file could be the difference between hundreds of thousands of dollars in life-time income. For married individuals, these decisions are even more critical because they affect the lives of two people instead of one.
- A well-designed Social Security filing strategy can increase a family's total lifetime income benefits **by more than $230,000** on average. Recent studies show that optimizing the timing and method of claiming benefits is key to achieving this significant increase, highlighting the value of strategic retirement planning. [3]
- Not all financial professionals are qualified to give you advice about when and how to file for your Social Security. Look for additional training and designations that educate and certify that someone has been properly trained with what may be your most important retirement decision to get right.

Most people are never exposed to these things, but you are holding this book, so you're ahead of the game. **The Social Security**

3 Based on 2023 data on Social Security optimization strategies, which have shown that households can increase their lifetime benefits by an average of $231,963 through proper planning. Source: "New Tool Creates a Seamless Transition from Social Security Optimization to Annuity Illustration and Proposal," LifeYield, 2023. Retrieved from https://www.lifeyield.com/new-tool-creates-a-seamless-transition-from-social-security-optimization-to-annuity-illustration-and-proposal/.

Administration is legally prohibited from giving you financial planning advice about claiming strategies because of all the areas this one decision affects. They cannot help you to get an optimal strategy for your family. In fact, I hear from people every year that were told incorrect or incomplete information from the Social Security Administration.

THE SHOCKING FINDINGS FROM THE OIG STUDY

In 2018, the Office of the Inspector General for the Social Security Administration collected data from a random sample of 50 beneficiaries who were applying for their Social Security benefit. Their findings? I'll quote the report:

"We did not find any evidence SSA had informed claimants of the option to delay their retirement application when they applied for benefits, as required."[4]

This resulted in a lot of people losing out on a lot of money.

- An estimated 11,123 people would have been eligible for a *higher* monthly benefit amount had they delayed their retirement application until age 70.
- The Social Security Administration underpaid about $131.8 million to 9,224 beneficiaries who were age 70 and older.
- The OIG estimates that the Social Security Administration will underpay an additional 1,899 beneficiaries who were under age 70 about $9.8 million, annually, beginning in the year they attain age 70.

My point in sharing this with you is that SSA representatives may not always provide full information, making it crucial to be proactive in understanding your options. You aren't going to be handed a clear path on how to do this, and you need to make the best decision

4 Higher Benefits for Dually Entitled Window(er)s Had They Delayed Applying for Retirement Benefits," Acting Inspector General, Feb.14, 2018, Social Security Administration.

possible. There are just too many exceptions, rules, considerations, filing strategies and circumstances. If you want to get this decision right, you have to think about the long game of retirement.

ADD WATER AND MIX FOR AN INSTANT RETIREMENT?

We live in an era when immediate gratification is practically at our fingertips. We can send messages across thousands of miles with the press of a button; stocks are traded on Wall Street at lightning speed; we have instant breakfasts, quick lunches and microwave dinners. So, you might wonder, where can you get an instant retirement?

I wish it were that easy, but if you want to do it right, it's going to take some effort. In most cases, the quick-and-easy solutions that rely on rules of thumb and ready-made answers to tough retirement questions are not one-size-fits-all. Neither are they instant. They require careful coordination of many puzzle pieces.

Your decision about when and how to file for Social Security is about money, yes, but it's also about a lot of other things including not only financial assets, but lifestyle goals, health considerations and family dynamics. Given that Social Security may make up 50% or more of this income, it deserves your focused attention.

Retirement isn't an event that lasts a few hours, days or even years. It goes on for decades. That's why your filing decision should not be made alone in a vacuum. You have to look at all the pieces that make up your retirement—and your life.

Generally speaking, we can break those pieces down into three different types of categories:

HUMAN CONSIDERATIONS

- Health
- Job satisfaction

- Spouse/who you want to live with
- Family/who you want to be near (or faraway from)
- Housing/where you want to live
- Desires/hopes and dreams

FINANCIAL CONSIDERATIONS

- Your 401(k), IRA, 403(b) or other retirement accounts
- Investment and brokerage accounts
- Life insurance policies
- Pensions
- Annuities
- Other sources of income such as rental properties
- Taxes

RISK FACTORS THAT MAY BE OUTSIDE OF YOUR CONTROL

- Longevity (how long you will live)
- Market risk
- Inflation
- Liquidity needs
- Frailty issues
- Long-term care

You might have other factors that are weighing on your mind. If you do, they also need to be put on the table with all the other pieces so that you can make the best possible decision. You might want to leave your job early where you are earning $85,000 a year; you might want to get a divorce and buy an RV; you might want to retire early and open an art studio; you might want to work part-time during retirement for non-financial reasons.

Whenever you make these human choices, you also need to understand the financial impact, both for the short term and the long term, and you need to examine the risk to your retirement plan. In so many cases, I see how an unprepared choice today becomes a major financial issue in the future. Nobody wants to run out of money too soon. I urge you to work with someone who can help you get a coordination strategy that takes into consideration ALL the pieces of your retirement puzzle.

You've worked hard your entire life to get to where you are today. You deserve the maximum amount of benefits that you are entitled to. The best way to achieve this is to make a filing decision that is coordinated with your other income amounts, your taxes and your non-financial concerns, such as your health, family and your own desires, so that you can get a strategy that works to give you efficiency and effectiveness, with the maximum benefits for minimum risks.

CREATE A COORDINATED FILING STRATEGY

Creating a coordinated filing strategy is one of the most impactful decisions you can make for your retirement. A well-thought-out strategy can help your portfolio last longer, increase your lifetime income, and reduce your tax burden. By aligning your Social Security benefits with your other income sources and retirement goals, you ensure that your financial plan is as efficient and effective as possible.

Financial professionals who are trained in Social Security optimization can be invaluable in this process. These experts use proprietary software to analyze hundreds of different filing dates, claiming strategies, and tax repercussions.[5] The result is a detailed report that projects what your financial situation might look like 10, 20, and even 30 years into retirement. This isn't just about maximizing your Social Security benefits—it's about integrating those benefits into your overall retirement plan to achieve your long-term goals.

5 The Retirement Analysis gives estimates based on your actual Social Security earning record. Please keep in mind that these are just estimates. We can't provide your actual benefit amount until you apply for benefits. And that amount may be different from the estimates provided.

To create a truly coordinated filing strategy, consider using our Social Security Clarity Analysis™ service at SocialSecurityClarity.com/analyze

But even with a coordinated strategy, there are still pitfalls that many retirees face. In the next chapter, we'll discuss the second major mistake: failing to understand the tax implications of your Social Security benefits. This is another area where a lack of awareness can lead to costly errors, and we'll explore how to avoid this common trap.

For additional tools and resources to assist with creating a coordinated filing strategy for your household, visit SocialSecurityClarity.com/resources.

RECAP & WHAT'S NEXT

In this chapter, we explored how creating a coordinated filing strategy is one of the most impactful decisions you can make for your retirement. By aligning your Social Security benefits with your other income sources and retirement goals, you can enhance your financial confidence.

In the next chapter, we'll dive into the second major mistake: failing to understand the tax implications of your Social Security benefits. This is another area where a lack of awareness can lead to costly errors, and we'll explore how to avoid this common trap.

CHAPTER 2

PAYING MORE THAN YOUR SHARE OF TAXES

Gary and Marie have an IRA that has been growing tax-deferred for the last 35 years. They are proud of what they've accumulated, but they're also worried about running out of money. While they know that this money wasn't taxed before it was put away, they don't really think that much about taxes. Once a year they meet with their CPA. He tells them about all the itemized deductions they qualify for, and then they pay their taxes and forget about them until next year.

What they do know about taxes is pretty straightforward: They want to pay as little as possible, and they want to pay them later, not now. This philosophy makes up the bulk of their tax strategy. They have also heard that they should take their withdrawals from their regular accounts first so that their tax-deferred accounts can continue to grow as long as possible.

To that end, Gary and Marie file early for Social Security so that they can withdraw as little as possible from their IRA. They each take a 25% benefit reduction of their Social Security income, but they get the money right away. The rest of what they need for income they pull from their IRA. At the end of the year, they go once again to see their CPA about their taxes.

Their CPA tells them that because of their provisional income, their adjusted gross income qualifies them for an income tax bracket of 25%. This is a surprise to them because they thought that during retirement, they would be in a lower tax bracket. Without really understanding why, they shell out just over $10,000 for taxes.

Meanwhile, their neighbors Jack and Beverly are also receiving the exact same amount of income every year; however, they worked with a financial professional that helped them to coordinate their income distribution planning, Social Security optimization, and tax strategy before filing for their Social Security. They qualified for no other kind of filing strategy, but because they had a better coordinated strategy, they are paying only $2,000 in taxes while receiving the exact same income! Over the course of the next 20 years, these two neighbors continue into their retirement, both of them receiving the same annual income. The only difference is that Jack and Beverly pay $160,000 LESS in taxes, and as a result, their investment portfolio lasts a lot longer. Another way of looking at this is that over 20 years, Gary and Marie paid $160,000 MORE in taxes than necessary due to suboptimal Social Security claiming - money that could have funded their grandson's college tuition or enhanced their retirement lifestyle. Jack and Beverly feel much more confident about not running out of money than their neighbors Gary and Marie.

It can be frustrating as a tax paying citizen to hear phrases such as *provisional income* and *adjusted gross income* and realize that these words have something to do with whether or not you'll run out of money. It's enough to make a person want to scream! Putting together an integrated retirement strategy is a complicated puzzle, and taxes are a vital component. They might not be fun, but planning for them instead of just paying them can add years and dollars to your income and peace of mind.

Fast Fact: Implementing a tax-advantaged strategy has the potential to significantly increase your overall portfolio balance, with some models suggesting gains of over 16%.

Having a tax-advantaged strategy is a big part of having a successful Social Security strategy. The two neighbors in our story both received the exact same retirement income. They both saved pretax money in their IRAs, and they both received their Social Security benefits, but the different characteristics of the sources of income and the order in which they *spent* those dollars made all the difference in how long their money lasted. The couple who saved over $160,000 in taxes qualified for no other claiming strategy. They also didn't have a side hustle or get lucky in the stock market. Their portfolio lasted longer for this simple reason: ***They made more money by spending less on taxes.*** You can learn how to do that, too. This chapter is here to show you how.

DODGE THE TAX TORPEDO BY FLIPPING THE SCRIPT

A lot of people like Gary and Marie in our story above follow the conventional wisdom of waiting as long as possible before spending the money in their IRA. Here's the thing, though: Uncle Sam has a time clock ticking on that pot of money. Once you reach the age of Required Minimum Distributions (RMDs), you no longer have a choice about whether or not you spend it; you MUST spend it.

The SECURE Act of 2019 increased the RMD age from 70 ½ to 72. Just a few years later, The SECURE Act of 2022 again delayed this age from 72 to 73, and it will increase again to age 75 in 2033 (assuming no new changes come into play).

The IRS calculates your RMD amount each year based on the total sum of money in the IRA pot and the number of years you likely have left in which to spend it. What typically happens is that while waiting to spend it, this money grows, thus increasing your tax obligation and the amount of your RMD. Once people hit RMD age, they also get hit with what we in the industry calls the tax torpedo. It hits with a stealth that most retirees don't expect, and the shock waves can give you three bad surprises:

- **An increase in the taxes you have to pay:** Your income goes up because of your RMD, and for some people, it's enough to push them over the threshold into the next income tax bracket
- **A decrease in the amount of Social Security you get to keep:** Because your income goes up, the amount of taxes you pay on your Social Security income can also go up, which means you're giving more of your Social Security benefit to Uncle Sam.
- **And the cherry on the sundae:** Even the income you receive from tax-free bonds counts against you.

Jack and Beverly in our story worked with a retirement planning specialist who understood how to help someone dodge this tax torpedo. Instead of filing early for their benefit, he advised them to pull out the money from their IRA account *first*, reducing the income source taxed the highest to grow an income source that's lower taxed with a cost-of-living adjustment.

Today, they receive a *larger* percentage of their income from Social Security, and they pull out a smaller amount from their IRAs. Their provisional income is lower than that of Gary and Marie, and so their adjusted gross income puts them in a lower, 12% tax bracket. Because of this strategy, their tax bill is just over $2,000 a year.

This story was based on actual people who paid their taxes based on the tax brackets and rates from 2016 and 2017. Here is what the income thresholds look like for someone retired today:

2025 TAX BRACKETS AND RATES

Rate	For married individual filing joint returns, taxable income over	For heads of households, taxable income over
10%	$0 – $23,850	$0 – $11,925
12%	$23,850	$11,925
22%	$96,950	$48,475
24%	$206,700	$103,350
32%	$394,600	$197,300
35%	$501,050	$250,525
37%	$751,600	$626,350

Source: https://www.irs.gov/newsroom/irs-releases-tax-inflation-adjustments-for-tax-year-2025

Want to know if you're in the path of the tax torpedo? Get a personalized tax impact analysis at SocialSecurityClarity.com/analyze.

WHAT YOU MIGHT NOT KNOW ABOUT TAXES DURING RETIREMENT

While paying your taxes later might sound like a good idea, in reality, it might cost you a lot less to pay them now. The money growing in your IRA or 401(k) grows protected from taxes. It isn't a question of whether or not you have to pay taxes on the money; it's a question of WHEN.

As I mentioned earlier, Uncle Sam has rules about when you can spend this money. You may not spend it before the age of 59 ½, or you will be penalized with a 10% tax (with a few exceptions). However, once you retire and reach that age, you can spend as much as you want without penalty. **There is also no rule that says you must wait until age 73 before withdrawing from your IRA.** Spending it early just may help you dodge the tax torpedo.

If you retire early and continue to let the money in your IRA grow, it could realistically double in 7-10 years. While that might sound like a reason to celebrate, remember that Uncle Sam is standing by, waiting for his share. You've basically just made your tax problem twice as big, and the tax rates will most likely be higher in 10 years than they are today. When the IRS says you must take out the RMD, you also have to pay tax on the RMD whether it's money you need or not.

Many couples like Jack and Beverly in our story find that spending more of their IRA money *early* during retirement is able to extend the life of their portfolio. One of the reasons this happens is because the money you receive from Social Security is taxed at a lower rate. The larger the percentage of income made up of this lower taxed source of income (compared to pre-tax retirement accounts), the smaller your total tax bill.

HOW TO REDUCE YOUR RETIREMENT TAX RATE

Every dollar that you take out from a traditional IRA has to be taxed at ordinary income tax rates because you didn't pay tax on this money when you saved it. Every dollar you receive from Social Security, however, is NOT taxed. As much as 100% of this income and at least 15% can be received tax-free! Furthermore, only 50% of this income is used to calculate your provisional *income*.

Considering this, it might make sense to build a tax strategy around the goal of receiving as much income as possible at the lower tax rate for as long as possible. Because only 50% of your Social Security income is counted in the provisional income formula, you can spend twice as much Social Security income as compared with IRA income before hitting the taxable income threshold.

The Social Security Administration uses a formula in order to determine how much of your Social Security benefit will be taxed. This formula calculates your combined income by looking at your *adjusted gross income*. Your *provisional income* also comes into play.

- Your *adjusted gross income* (AGI) is your total gross income minus specific deductions.
- Your *provisional income* is your adjusted gross income before Social Security benefits plus any tax-free interest income. (This includes interest from municipal bonds and tax-exempt bond mutual funds.)

Some people have to pay federal taxes on the income they receive from Social Security, while other people don't. The SSA has set certain income thresholds to determine how much of your income will be taxed. To understand how much of your income will be taxed, you first have to understand how Social Security calculates your combined income.

Your *combined income* is:

Your adjusted gross income before Social Security benefits

+ any non-taxable interest income

+ ½ of your Social Security income.

Add those three things up, and *voila*, you have your combined income according to Social Security.

HOW MUCH OF YOUR BENEFIT WILL BE TAXED?

While all of the money you take out of your IRA will be taxed, not all of your Social Security money will be taxed. Every year, the SSA establishes thresholds for your combined income. There are three tiers to these income thresholds.

As of 2025, those tiers look like this:

- **If you file a federal tax return as an "individual"** and your combined income is:
  - Less than $25,000, you may not have to pay any income taxes on your Social Security benefit

  - Between $25,000 and $34,000, you may have to pay income tax on up to 50% of your benefit
  - More than $34,000, up to 85% of your benefit may be taxable.
- **If you file a joint return,** and you and your spouse have a *combined income* that is
  - Less than $32,000, you may not have to pay any income taxes on your Social Security benefits
  - Between $32,000 and $44,000, you may have to pay income tax on up to 50% of your benefits
  - More than $44,000, up to 85% of your benefits may be taxable.
- **If you are married and file a separate tax return**, you will probably pay taxes on your benefits.

Fast Fact: No one pays federal income tax on more than 85% of their Social Security benefits based on the rules by the IRS.

Will your RMDs throw you into the path of the tax torpedo? That's a question you'll want to answer *before* you determine the best time to file for your Social Security benefit. Having a tax-advantaged strategy can get you more lifetime income from Social Security income, years of portfolio longevity and fewer tax obligations. Consult with a financial professional who has training in this area, or you just might find yourself with a retirement that blows up.

For a deeper dive into coordinating RMDs with Social Security, see Chapter 10.

RECAP & WHAT'S NEXT

In this chapter, we discussed the importance of tax planning in relation to your Social Security benefits. Understanding how your income sources interact with taxes can help you preserve your retirement income and maintain financial confidence.

To help you apply these principles, use the **Social Security Tax Strategy Guide™** at the end of this chapter. This worksheet will guide you through evaluating the tax implications of your Social Security benefits.

As we move forward, we'll explore another common mistake: not considering the financial impact on your spouse when making Social Security decisions.

SOCIAL SECURITY TAX STRATEGY GUIDE™

EXAMINE THE TAX TREATMENT OF YOUR SOCIAL SECURITY BENEFIT

If you have a large pre-tax bucket of money made up of 401(k)s, IRAs or 403(b)s, then you might be in the path of the tax torpedo. To find out if you would benefit from income distribution and tax strategy planning, go through the following questions and record your answers. This can help you get a clearer picture of where you stand: in the path of the torpedo or in the clear.

IDENTIFY YOUR AGI:

Your adjusted gross income is your gross income minus adjustments. You may locate your AGI on your tax return. Alternatively, you can call the IRS telephone assistance line at 1-800-829-1040. Once the IRS verifies who you are, they may give you your prior-year AGI over the phone.

Your AGI is: ______________________________

LOOK AT YOUR RMD:

If you have a traditional IRA, you must start taking your Required Minimum Distributions (RMDs) each year beginning with the year you reach your required beginning age. The SECURE Act 2.0 changed the RMD start age based on your birth year:

- ☐ If you were born between 1951 and 1959, you must begin RMDs at age 73.
- ☐ If you were born in 1960 or later, you must begin RMDs at age 75.
- ☐ The RMD for each year is calculated by dividing the IRA account balance as of December 31 of the previous year by the

applicable distribution period or life expectancy, as determined by the IRS. Your income withdrawals may already satisfy your RMD requirement. Check with your financial professional.

My RMD date is: ___________________________________

Note: You can estimate your RMD by dividing your retirement account balance by your life expectancy factor. Or visit SocialSecurityClarity.com/resources for free RMD calculator resources.

My RMD is: ___________________________________

My spouse's is: ___________________________________

With your RMD(s), your new AGI at age 73 or 75 is or will be:

____

CALCULATE YOUR COMBINED INCOME:

Your *combined income* is a total of your AGI before Social Security benefits + any non-taxable interest + HALF of your Social Security benefit.

Note: Nontaxable interest is typically reported on line 8b of your 1040 or 1040A tax form.

Now:

__________ + __________ + __________ = Your combined income

Your AGI Before SSB   Your Non-Taxable Interest   ½ of your SS income

After RMDs begin (at age 73 or 75):

__________ + __________ + __________ = Your combined income

Your AGI Before SSB   Your Non-Taxable Interest   ½ of your SS income

My combined income now is: ___________________

My combined income after RMDs begin is: ___________

Calculate how much of your Social Security income will be taxed: Locate your filing status and place a checkmark in the circle that represents your combined income. Be sure to record both your income now and your income later if your RMD will affect your AGI.

If you file a federal tax return as an "individual" and your *combined income* is:

- Less than $25,000, you may not have to pay any income taxes on your Social Security benefit
- Between $25,000 and $34,000, you may have to pay income tax on up to 50% of your benefit
- More than $34,000, up to 85% of your benefit may be taxable.

My Social Security income will be taxed at ____________%.

If you file a joint return, and you and your spouse have a *combined income* that is

- Less than $32,000, you may not have to pay any income taxes on your Social Security benefits
- Between $32,000 and $44,000, you may have to pay income tax on up to 50% of your benefits
- More than $44,000, up to 85% of your benefits may be taxable.

My Social Security income will be taxed at ____________%.

Are you happy with the current outlook for your retirement taxes, both now and after RMD age? Please mark one:

☐ Yes ☐ No

If you marked No, this is your wake-up call. Find a trained financial professional who is a specialist in retirement income planning and ask them to design an income distribution and tax strategy, ideally before you file for your Social Security.

For a deeper dive into how taxes and spousal benefits interact with Social Security, visit SocialSecurityClarity.com/resources. You can access worksheets and calculators that make it easy to visualize how these strategies might play out in your own retirement plan.

CHAPTER 3

ROBBING YOUR SPOUSE

WHAT HAPPENS WHEN A SPOUSE DIES

Bob thought he was in a good position to retire early because he would receive a benefit check for the rest of his life. He filed for Social Security as soon as he retired. At age 63 and three months, his benefit was $1,833 a month, and he thought that was pretty good. What he didn't think about was how this decision affected his wife, Mary.

Mary had stayed home with their three kids when they were young, and then she worked part time as a librarian. Her pension and Social Security benefits were much smaller than Bob's, but when everything was added together, they did all right. Their total combined household income was $58,286 a year. Their golden years were peaceful and fun. Mary kept busy by volunteering at their granddaughter's school, and Bob enjoyed his Monday and Thursday golf games with the guys. When Bob passed away at the age of 75, Mary was only 70 years old. She was stunned by his death, and at a loss as to how she would carry on. What made everything so much more difficult was that her income had suddenly and permanently been cut by over 38%.

She had to sell the house and move away from a place she knew and loved. She had to give up her time volunteering at the school. Everything good about her life changed because even though all of *her monthly bills had stayed the same, she found herself with an income that was $22,190 less.*

Mary in our story is based on an actual woman who came to see me for the first time after her husband had died. She had no idea how or why her income had suddenly dropped. This is completely normal. Income in a household drops often by as much as half when a spouse dies. The second thing that is often not planned for is the Double Whammy effect sometimes referred to as The Widow Penalty that occurs when the household income decreases, but the tax burden actually goes up from becoming a single tax filer instead of married! All Mary knew was that it was hard. She and Bob had always taken care of each other. He was a smart man who loved his family. He remembered their anniversary and they often held hands when they went out on dates. She didn't understand why he would "do this to her."

The combination of reduced household income and higher single-filer tax rates creates what we call the 'Widow's Penalty Double Whammy.' To understand how this could impact your household and explore possible alternative strategies, get a personalized survivor benefit analysis at SocialSecurityClarity.com/protect-spouse

Unfortunately, I had no answers for Mary. The reality is that it's normal. Most couples never get around to planning for what happens when a spouse dies, even though it's a certainty. If you're married, this chapter might be the most important information to understand, and talking through what is the plan when a spouse dies needs to be added as an action item to address.

Bob in our story failed to consider his spouse, both when claiming his pension and when filing for his Social Security. Does that make him inconsiderate? His wife, Mary, might have a few thoughts about that.

The associate director for research at the Center for Retirement Research at Boston College looked into the situation and also shared his group's findings in a research paper titled, *Why Do Married Men Claim Social Security Benefits So Early? Ignorance or Caddishness?*

But what is caddishness? The term often implies selfish, rude, or deceitful actions, especially in how someone treats others. In my experience, the result of this kind of shortsightedness comes down to a simple lack of awareness. People are busy with their careers, families, and lives and get around to creating a plan for the death of a spouse. I bring these things up not to induce fear but to bring awareness to what happens in these scenarios so that you can now be better equipped to plan for them. Indeed, the results of the study reportedly found "no association between early claiming and caddishness." Mary would probably agree with that.

While fewer individuals are claiming benefits as soon as they are eligible in recent years, nearly half of all men claim before their full retirement age as of 2022 according to the SSA[6]. They don't stop to consider the benefit amounts they *could* have reached by waiting. Married people have an additional incentive to wait before claiming. When one spouse passes away, the surviving spouse may receive the higher of the two checks. It only makes sense to let that check get as big as it can get.

In our story, Bob might have left his wife with a survivor benefit of $2,904 a month instead of $1,833 a month. My friend Thomas, who we talked about earlier in the introduction of this book, caused his wife to lose out on over $200,000 in lifetime benefits because he filed at a less than optimized time for his household. Let's take a look at why this happens, and what simple steps you can take to avoid unintentionally hurting the person that you love.

DEALING WITH DEATH

The death of a spouse during retirement can cause more than just emotional hardship; it can lead to significant financial strain for the next 10–20 years of the survivor's life. A recent analysis by the U.S. Census Bureau shows that a significant majority of older adults living

6 https://www.ssa.gov/policy/docs/statcomps/supplement/2023/6b.html#table6.b5

below the poverty line are women.[7] What's interesting is that more than half of these women were NOT poor before the death of their husbands. This happens for three reasons:

- Women tend to live longer than men.
- Most women are younger than their husbands.
- The income women earn during their working years tends to be lower than men's.

All three of these reasons applied to Mary in our story. Her pension was only $500 a month—a fraction of her husband's—and she was fortunate to even have one given today's trends. When her husband passed away, she lost Bob's pension entirely. She was then eligible for the higher of their two Social Security checks. Bob's PIA was $2,200, but since he took his benefit at age 63, it was permanently reduced to $1,833, which also became Mary's survivor benefit. When she switched to the survivor benefit, she lost her own check, resulting in a significant reduction in her total income. This is not uncommon; many widows experience up to a 50% drop in income, while household expenses typically decrease by only 20% after a spouse's death.

This makes sense if you think about it. All of the main living expenses stay about the same. It's kind of like getting a hotel room: Usually, the rates for one- and two-person occupancy are exactly the same. So, who is to blame?

HOW TO AVOID ROBBING YOUR SPOUSE

Studies examining the cause of these income cuts point the finger of blame at the higher-earning spouse. Let me put it to you like this:

It is up to the primary breadwinner of the household to wake up to the fact that his or her filing decision will have a HUGE impact on the well-being of the surviving spouse.

7 U.S. Census Bureau, Current Population Reports, Poverty in the United States: 2022, U.S. Government Publishing Office, Washington, DC, September 2023.

It's really pretty simple. If you're earning more money than your spouse, then you have a responsibility to look at the bigger picture of how the income situation would change should you be the first one to pass away. It isn't that hard to see when you compare and model multiple scenarios that can often produce a significantly higher lifetime income and protect the lives of both spouses.

While the facts might seem to conspire unfairly against the financial security of women, there are things that you can do to prepare. Model your retirement timeline and plan for your cash flow during retirement both while both spouses are alive, and also when a spouse dies.

Fast Fact: In 2022, the median income for women aged 65 and older was approximately 65% of that of men in the same age group, with women earning about $24,630 annually compared to $37,430 for men.[8]

The most common mistake is that the higher wage earner files early, reducing both their own benefit and the survivor benefit for their spouse for the remainder of their lifetime. For example, if the higher earner with a Full Retirement Age (FRA) of age 67 files at age 62, they receive 70% of their Primary Insurance Amount (PIA), and if they pass away, their spouse will receive that same reduced amount as a survivor benefit. The closer to FRA the higher earner waits to file, the closer both their benefit and the survivor benefit will be to 100% of their PIA.

Fast Fact: How much your family can get from Social Security depends on your average lifetime earnings. The more you earned, the more their benefits will be.

---

8 https://pensionrights.org/resource/income-received-by-different-groups/

The system is set up to help you take care of your family; Social Security is designed to provide comprehensive protection for American workers and their families against the loss of earnings. The key is to spend time navigating this benefit. Getting this wrong has high stakes for you and the person you care about the most.

IF YOU ARE MARRIED, STOP BEFORE YOU FILE AND THINK ABOUT YOUR SPOUSE

Most people—even smart, nice, successful people—don't stop to think about the significant drop in income that can occur with the death of a spouse. It's essential to take a moment out of your busy life to understand the rules that apply in this situation. Retirement is a cash-flow game, and having a well-thought-out income plan, grounded in mathematical certainty rather than luck, is critical for a successful retirement.

We need to ensure that the pieces of our financial puzzle are put together in the right way so that our income continues to exceed our expenses, even after the death of a spouse. Being strategic with your benefits could be the difference between maintaining your lifestyle versus having to reduce it—or worse, going back to work.

RECAP & WHAT'S NEXT

In this chapter, we highlighted the critical importance of considering your spouse's financial well-being when making Social Security decisions. Coordinating benefits to ensure your spouse's long-term financial confidence can make a significant difference in retirement.

To support you in this effort, complete the **Spousal Social Security Checklist™** included at the end of this chapter. This worksheet will help you assess how your decisions affect your spouse's future income.

Next, we'll discuss the potential pitfalls of working while claiming Social Security and how to avoid reducing your benefits unnecessarily.

SPOUSAL SOCIAL SECURITY CHECKLIST™

5 QUESTIONS TO ASK IF YOU ARE MARRIED AND WORRIED ABOUT TAKING CARE OF YOUR SPOUSE:

Below, you'll find a worksheet designed to help you assess and plan for your spouse's financial future with Social Security. This tool will guide you through the essential steps to help ensure that your spouse is well taken care of, even if you're no longer there to provide support. It's an invaluable resource that can make all the difference in your retirement planning.

1. **Have I investigated the spousal options for my pension benefits?**

   Amount of full pension benefit: ______________________________
   Reduced pension benefit option #1 for myself: ______________
   ____
   Reduced pension benefit option #2 for myself: ______________
   Pension benefit option for spousal benefit #1: ______________
   Pension benefit option for spousal benefit #2: ______________

2. **Have I investigated life insurance options to replace any pension income?**

   Amount of pension income that needs to be replaced: ______
   Death benefit on life insurance option #1: ________________
   Death benefit on life insurance option #2: ________________

3. **Have I maximized my Social Security benefit to understand how much my spouse will receive upon my death?**

   PIA of higher-earning spouse: ____________________________
   Survivor benefit filing option #1: _________________________
   Survivor benefit filing option #2: _________________________
   Survivor benefit filing option #3: _________________________
   Survivor benefit filing option #4: _________________________

Survivor benefit filing option #5: ______________________________

4. **What income gap will I or my spouse have to fill once one of us passes away?**

   Household income gap amount (as calculated in Chapter 10): ______________________________

   Income gap should I pass away first (calculate the loss of the lower Social Security check and any pension income or single-life only annuity income connected to the individual): ______________

   Income gap for myself should my spouse pass away first (calculate the loss of the lower Social Security check and any pension income or single-life only annuity income connected to the individual): ______________________________

5. **How much will my spouse or I receive in income every month before and after one of us passes away?**

   Total amount of household income during retirement (pension amounts, Social Security and known sources of income for both you and your spouse): ______________________________

Survivor Income for Spouse:

Amount of the highest Social Security check: ______________
Pension amount (if any): ______________________________
Guaranteed source of income option #1: ______________
Guaranteed source of income option #2: ______________
Guaranteed source of income option #3: ______________
Total amount of income for survivor per month: ____________

Survivor Income for Yourself:

Amount of the highest Social Security check: ______________
Pension amount (if any): ______________________________
Guaranteed source of income option #1: ______________
Guaranteed source of income option #2: ______________
Guaranteed source of income option #3: ______________

Total amount of income for survivor per month: ___________

For a comprehensive checklist covering all aspects of survivor benefit protection, see The Social Security Clarity Master Checklist™, available as a downloadable PDF at SocialSecurityClarity.com/resources.

CHAPTER 4

SHOOTING YOURSELF IN THE FOOT WHILE WORKING LIKE A DOG

*Ginny had a Primary Insurance Amount (PIA) of **$1,000** a month. She started taking her Social Security benefit at age 63 because she knew she was old enough, and she thought, why not create a little breathing room and go ahead and get the extra money? She wanted to retire, but she felt she needed to keep earning money to make ends meet, save for retirement, and help pay for her grandson's college tuition.*

*When Ginny got her first Social Security check in the mail, however, she was shocked. Instead of the **$800** she was expecting (her monthly benefit amount after the age-based reduction), Ginny received a check for **$383.***

"This has to be a mistake!" she thought. But when she called up the Social Security Administration, she was told that no mistake had been made. This was the benefit she was entitled to.

It turns out that Ginny was the one who made the mistake on the day that she filed for Social Security. Fortunately, she came in to talk to me right away before 12 months had passed, and Ginny was able to withdraw her filing decision. (She did have to pay back the benefit she received up to that point.)

She was glad she did because she had filed early without understanding the rules when it comes to claiming her benefit before full retirement age. She didn't realize that her benefit would be reduced and that the reduction for filing early would last for the rest of her life. She also didn't know she would be penalized $1 for every $2 that she earned above the earnings threshold while working!

From an educational and economic standpoint, this is one area where what you don't know CAN hurt you. Here is what you need to know about working while claiming Social Security.

CAN YOU LEGALLY COLLECT SOCIAL SECURITY BEFORE YOU RETIRE?

You can legally collect Social Security before you retire and stop working, but in order to get the most out of your benefit, you'll want to know the rules. Not all workers will be penalized, and for some people, working longer will only *increase* your future benefit amount.

There are two factors that determine whether or not your benefit will be reduced:

1. The amount of money you earn at work.
2. Your full retirement age.

Some people *need* to work while claiming their benefit. If this is you, please don't stop reading this chapter until you reach the end. The news isn't all bad! If you're penalized for working while receiving your benefit, you just might receive the money back in the form of higher benefit checks later.

Here are the rules for working while claiming your benefit:

IF YOU ARE UNDER FULL RETIREMENT AGE AND WORKING

Social Security has different rules depending on your relationship to your full retirement age. If you are not going to reach full retirement age during the calendar year, then the SSA will deduct $1 for every $2 that you earn above the annual limit. The annual limit for 2025 is $23,400.

What does that look like? Ginny in our story had a Primary Insurance Amount (PIA) of $1,000, but because she filed at the age of 63, her benefit was reduced to $800 a month. This was a permanent reduction that would go into effect for the rest of her life. On top of that decrease, Ginny was also losing money because she was working while claiming benefits. Ginny had earned $33,400 that year, which was $10,000 over the limit. Her benefit was reduced by $5,000 ($1 for every $2 that she earned over the limit.) She should have received $9,600 for the year from Social Security; instead, Ginny was going to receive only $4,600, or $383 a month, an amount that she realized wasn't worth it. She would rather pick up more hours at work, wait a few years longer and let her benefit mature. By waiting just three years, she can receive her full benefit amount of $12,000 annually.

Fast Fact: If your earnings will be over the limit during the year that you retire, don't worry! There is a special rule that applies to earnings for the year that you retire. This rule means that if Social Security considers you retired, they will pay you a FULL Social Security check regardless of your income earnings from work up to that point in the year.

IF YOU REACH FULL RETIREMENT AGE AND YOU ARE WORKING

The year you reach your full retirement age, the Social Security Administration uses a different formula with higher income thresholds to calculate your benefit reduction. They will deduct $1 for every $3 you earn above the specified limit, which is adjusted annually. For 2025, that amount is $62,160. Additionally, the penalty applies only during the months before you reach full retirement age, meaning that once you hit your FRA, you can earn any amount without reducing your Social Security benefits.

For example, if you earn $66,000 in 2025 and reach full retirement age in September, with an earnings limit of $62,160 for the months before September, your income would exceed the limit by $3,480. Consequently, your Social Security benefit would be reduced by $1,280, which is $1 for every $3 over the limit. This reduction would be applied to your benefits from January through August, lowering your monthly benefit by approximately $160. Starting in September, when you reach full retirement age, you would receive your full benefit of $800 per month without any further reductions.

Fast Fact: When Social Security calculates how much to deduct from your benefits, they only look at your job wages or net profits if you're self-employed. They do NOT look at bonuses, commissions, vacation pay, pensions, annuities, investment income, interest or military or veteran retirement benefits.

IF YOU ARE PAST FULL RETIREMENT AGE AND WORKING

Beginning with the month that you reach full retirement age, there's a little-known loophole that allows you to legally collect Social Security even before you officially retire, with no penalty, no matter how much you earn. You may also work while receiving your survivor's benefits.

Every year that you work can delete the lower-earning years from your work history, potentially raising your monthly benefit amount. Why? The Social Security Administration reviews the records for all working recipients annually. If your earnings for the year are higher than one of the 35 years they used to previously calculate your benefit, then they will do the math all over again and recalculate. Furthermore, they will pay the increase retroactive to January of the year after you earned the money! If you don't need the income, however, it might not be in your best interest to file for your benefit if you're planning to work later. Waiting to file can increase your check, and the check of your spousal benefit if you're married.

WHAT IF YOU HAVE TO WORK?

Given today's increased life expectancies, working longer may be a way to boost both your savings and your Social Security benefit. These higher benefit amounts can make a huge difference to you and your family later in life, particularly if you have a spouse who will receive a survivor's benefit.

If you need the money from Social Security and you decide to file even though you are still working and not yet full retirement age, there is a silver lining: When Social Security penalizes you, they also give you the money back. Once you reach full retirement age, they recalculate your benefit amount to give you credit for any months you received a reduced benefit because of your work earnings.

They don't send you a big fat check for the total amount, however. They use it to increase your benefit, so the money is earned back gradually, typically over a period of 15 or so years. The Social Security Administration will send you a letter telling you about the increase so that you can know what to expect at full retirement age.

RECAP & WHAT'S NEXT

In this chapter, we covered how working while claiming Social Security can significantly impact the amount of money you receive. Understanding the rules can help you preserve your income and avoid permanent reductions.

To ensure you fully grasp the implications of working while claiming, fill out the **Earnings Impact Calculator™** provided at the end of this chapter. This tool will help you evaluate the effects of working on your benefits.

Next, we'll tackle the fifth and final major mistake: picking the wrong claiming strategy and how to correct it.

EARNINGS IMPACT CALCULATOR™

UNDERSTAND THE PENALTY IF YOU PLAN TO WORK WHILE CLAIMING YOUR SOCIAL SECURITY

This worksheet is designed to help you assess the potential impact of working while claiming your Social Security benefits. By understanding how your earnings can affect your benefit amount, you can make more informed decisions that will protect your financial future.

1. Enter your date of birth: ______________________________
2. Enter your estimated earnings from work: ________________

Note: If you reach your full retirement age this year, enter only the earnings you will earn before the month you reach FRA. The penalty does not apply once you reach FRA.

3. Your estimated monthly benefit from Social Security: ______
4. Is the current year the FIRST year you are receiving benefits?

   ☐ Yes ☐ No

5. Enter this information and submit your request to: **www.ssa.gov/OACT/COLA/RTeffect.html**
6. Your benefits will be reduced by (annual amount): _________

This calculator will help you determine the exact impact of working on your Social Security benefits. It's an invaluable tool for anyone considering working after filing for Social Security.

For more tools and resources, including a PDF download of this worksheet, visit SocialSecurityClarity.com/resources. You'll find additional resources to help you navigate these important decisions and maximize your Social Security benefits.

CHAPTER 5

PICKING THE WRONG CLAIMING STRATEGY (AND HOW TO CORRECT IT)

As we have seen in previous examples, having a well thought through claiming strategy is about determining the best option for you and your family. There are many rules and nuances to Social Security, and not all of them are widely known. Over the years, I have seen families increase their income by over $100,000 just by getting a strategy in place. If you are married, divorced or widowed especially, you may have many more options for filing than you realize.

UNDERSTANDING THEN TO UNDERSTAND NOW

Trying to figure out which strategies you might qualify for has gotten trickier since the Bipartisan Budget Act was passed in 2015. A lot of online articles written before that time are not dated, and so they have misinformation. Hopefully, this chapter will give you some clarity about what you can and cannot do.

Before the 2015 Bipartisan Budget Act, there used to be two loop-holes that allowed some married couples to bridge their income gaps while waiting for their Social Security benefits to grow. Both strategies involved an extra helping of spousal benefits. Although the strategies were complex, they did not require that both spouses be at full retirement age, nor did both spouses have to file for their own benefits in order to receive these benefits.

The old system allowed married people to file a restricted application for a spousal benefit at full retirement age, so they were able to build up retirement credits while still receiving a paycheck. Social Security closed this loophole by passing the deemed filing rule. Now, if you qualify for both a retirement benefit and a spousal benefit, when you apply for one, you are "deemed" to be filing for the other benefit as well. You don't even get to pick which benefit you will get. The Social Security Administration will pay you whichever benefit is higher.

3 EXCEPTIONS TO DEEMED FILING

The deemed filing rule doesn't apply to everybody. There are three exceptions, and if you fall under one of them, then you may still take advantage of a filing strategy that can help you get an additional income boost.

Keep in mind, however, that even these rules can change. New amendments are likely to be passed in order to keep the system viable, so if you do qualify for a strategy, the time to act is now. If you qualify, you'll be able to start one type of benefit, let the other benefit grow and then switch over to your new, larger benefit. This can greatly increase your total lifetime income.

The three exceptions to deemed filing are:

1. Individuals who are receiving a spousal benefit because they are caring for a child who is under the age of 16.
2. Individuals who are receiving a spousal benefit because they are caring for a child who is disabled.

3. Individuals who are entitled to a survivor's benefit in addition to their own benefit.

Being aware of these exceptions can be especially important for widows or widowers who are looking for ways to supplement their income. Using a restricted application, they may apply for their survivor's benefits and receive one check while waiting for their own check to grow. Conversely, they might also apply for their own benefit while letting their survivor's benefit mature.

Because the deemed filing rule does not apply to survivors, they can then switch over at age 70 to their benefit thereby receiving the higher check. They can let one check grow without having to forgo a current retirement income.

WHAT IF YOU QUALIFY FOR A STRATEGY, BUT YOU ALREADY FILED?

A lot of people come to me after they hear my Social Security Optimization class with a pained look on their face because they realize

They made a mistake. There is still hope! Take a look at the end of this chapter to see if you qualify for a do-over. Even if you don't want to go through all of the steps, you may still be eligible for "Option B."

Fast Fact: In 2010, the rules for withdrawing your Social Security application changed. Prior to that time, there was no time limit as to how long you could wait before changing your mind.

WHAT IF YOU DON'T QUALIFY FOR A STRATEGY?

Even if you don't qualify for some of these strategies, your strategy then becomes coordinating your benefits with your other distribution sources, the tax consequences, and other assets. Timing your taxes correctly and coordinating your benefits are such an important part of Social Security optimization that the first two chapters are dedicated to those strategies.

Optimizing Social Security is about getting your highest lifetime benefit amount in a way that fits with your lifestyle and your goals. To help you achieve this, we offer resources designed to simplify your decision-making process. Start with the Social Security Clarity Master Checklist™, available as a downloadable PDF. In just five minutes, you'll know the right questions to ask your financial professional, bringing you closer to finding your better way.

For an even more tailored approach, request a personalized analysis of your claiming strategies to match your unique situation. Visit SocialSecurityClarity.com/strategy to get started.

A ONE-TIME DO-OVER: WITHDRAW YOUR APPLICATION TO ENHANCE YOUR STRATEGY

When you file for your Social Security benefit, this decision goes on to affect all the remaining years of your life, so mistakes in this area can be hard to forgive and forget. This step is for readers who have already filed for Social Security. If, during the course of reading this book, you have realized that you might have missed an opportunity or realize there might be a "better way," it might be possible for you to get a do-over so that you can boost your benefits. It might not be easy, and you must withdraw your application within 12 months of filing. I'd also recommend working with a financial professional who has experience in this area to get some guidance, because you're only allowed one do-over. Here is what you have to do:

- **Pay back all the benefits:** In order to get a do-over, Social Security requires that you pay back all of the benefits paid so far to you, including amounts withheld for taxes or Medicare premiums, which means you must pay back the gross amount, not just the amount of the actual check. (Don't worry—Social Security will do the math for you. I tell you this now so you can get a ballpark idea of what you owe.) You must also pay back all the benefits paid to anyone else who claimed based on your benefit. This includes your spouse, children or others whose ability to claim started on the day you filed your original application. (This does not apply to divorce benefits.)
- **Consent in writing:** All of the people who received benefits based on your claim—such as your spouse or children—must consent in writing to the withdrawal
- **Fill out Form SSA-521:** You have a 12-month window from the time of your original application during which you may submit Social Security Form SSA-521 to withdraw your application
- **Wait for notification:** After you send in Form SSA-521, the Social Security Administration will notify you of the exact amount that you'll need to repay in order to finalize the deal
- **Option B:** If you realize you're not able to meet all of these requirements, you do have one other option. Once you reach full retirement age but before age 70, you can choose to voluntarily suspend your payments. This will allow you to gain those delayed retirement benefits. You will not be able to receive any additional benefits while you wait for your benefit to grow, but once you claim on or before age 70, you can then reactivate your higher benefit amount.

RECAP & WHAT'S NEXT

In this chapter, we discussed the importance of choosing the right Social Security claiming strategy and how making the best choice for you can enhance your financial confidence throughout retirement.

To assist you in evaluating and selecting the optimal strategy for your household, complete the **Claiming Strategy Evaluation Worksheet™** provided at the end of this chapter. This tool is designed to guide you through comparing different claiming options.

In the next section, we'll move beyond identifying mistakes and focus on actionable solutions. Part 2 of this book will introduce a clear, step-by-step process designed to help you navigate Social Security decisions with confidence. Whether you're just starting to plan or need to adjust your current strategy, this process will guide you in optimizing your benefits for your specific situation.

CLAIMING STRATEGY EVALUATION WORKSHEET™

To help you evaluate and correct your Social Security claiming strategy, use the following checklist:

1. **Identify Your Eligibility**:
   - ☐ Have you reviewed your eligibility for spousal, survivor, or other specialized benefits?
   - ☐ Are you aware of any exceptions to the deemed filing rule that might apply to your situation?
2. **Understand the Impact of Coordination**:
   - ☐ How do your Social Security benefits interact with your other retirement income sources?
   - ☐ Have you considered the tax implications of your claiming strategy?
3. **Evaluate Your Options for a Do-Over**:
   - ☐ Are you within the 12-month window for a possible withdrawal? If so, are you prepared to repay all benefits received to date?
   - ☐ If withdrawing isn't an option, have you considered voluntary suspension to boost your benefits?
4. **Consult a Professional**:
   - ☐ Have you consulted with a financial professional who specializes in Social Security optimization?

For more tools and resources, including a downloadable PDF of this checklist, visit SocialSecurityClarity.com/resources.

PART 2

HOW TO DO IT RIGHT—THE PATH

"People often associate complexity with deeper meaning, when often after precious time has been lost, it is realized that simplicity is the key to everything."
- GARY HOPKINS

The rules for optimizing Social Security retirement income benefits can be complex; however, I believe it doesn't have to be complicated. With a clear process in place, it becomes manageable.In Part 1, we uncovered the biggest mistakes and pitfalls to avoid. Now, it's time to shift our focus to identifying a clear and actionable path forward. In part 2, we introduce the Social Security Path to Clarity™, my three-step approach designed to guide you toward an optimized claiming decision: Preparation, Evaluation, and Implementation.

INTRODUCING THE SOCIAL SECURITY PATH TO CLARITY™: A SIMPLE 1-2-3 PROCESS

1. **Preparation** - This initial step involves gathering key information about your individual financial and personal situation. By completing a detailed worksheet, you'll clarify your goals and assets, laying the groundwork for informed and strategic decision-making.

Mistake: Most people do not take the time to gather all the relevant information about their financial and personal situation. They are not clear on their goals, which results in missed opportunities.

---

2. **Evaluation** - In this critical step, viable Social Security claiming strategies and options are modeled for your specific circumstances. Each potential option is meticulously evaluated to identify the optimal strategy based on data-driven analysis tailored to your specific circumstances.

Mistake: Very few people take the time to properly model and compare viable Social Security claiming options for their household. They rely on anecdotal advice rather than data-driven analysis.

---

3. **Implementation** - This final step provides an implementation checklist that outlines the exact actions and deadlines needed to execute your chosen Social Security claiming strategy. By focusing on these implementation details, you can ensure a seamless transition to your optimized plan, avoiding delays or missed opportunities.

Mistake: Many people do not think about implementation details and deadlines. They do not have a clear plan for executing their strategy, which can lead to missed opportunities or delays.

Overall, most people do not spend adequate time on any of these three important steps. They do not prepare thoroughly, evaluate options carefully, or plan the implementation effectively. This often results in leaving tens of thousands of dollars to hundreds of thousands of dollars of lifetime benefits on the table from their Social Security benefits.

By embracing this three-step process—Preparation, Evaluation, Implementation—you'll be equipped with the critical information, tools, and a strategic plan necessary to make an optimized Social Security claiming decision, perfectly tailored to your household's unique situation.

Now that you have a roadmap, let's dive into the first step: Preparation. Together, we'll explore the foundational knowledge of the rules, strategies, and potential pitfalls that specifically apply to your household, setting the stage for informed and confident decision-making.

STEP 1

PREPARATION

"By failing to prepare, you are preparing to fail."
–BENJAMIN FRANKLIN

The Preparation step of The Social Security Path involves gathering key information about your individual situation through a comprehensive worksheet. This questionnaire delves into various aspects, such as your Social Security benefits, earnings history, existing pensions, marital status, and household dynamics.

The goal of the Preparation step is to identify all the relevant financial and personal 'puzzle pieces' that must be considered when crafting and modeling viable Social Security claiming strategies. This clarity sets the stage for a thorough and tailored Evaluation in the next step.

CHAPTER 6

BENEFIT BASICS WHO, WHAT AND WHEN

"Success is neither magical nor mysterious. Success is the natural consequence of consistently applying the basic fundamentals."

—JIM ROHN

Before we dig into the question of how much, we first need to understand the basics of who, what and when. We're going to talk about what Social Security is and what it isn't. Given the complexity of this program with its rules and exceptions to the rules, there are a few myths and misconceptions floating around out there about the program, and I'd like to clear a few things up right away.

What Social Security is NOT:

- A system you pay into where Uncle Sam puts your contributions via tax money into an account with your name on it so that when you retire, you can start pulling that money out. NOT
- A system designed to take more of your money than you will ever get back. NOT

- A benefit that is proportional to *exactly* how much money you made when you were working. NOT.

What Social Security IS:

- A federal insurance program that provides benefits to retired individuals, disabled workers, and their families, as well as survivors of deceased workers.
- A pay-as-you-go system where taxes paid by working people provide the benefits for those who are retired.
- **Social Security calculates your benefits based on your 35 highest-earning years**. To ensure that your past earnings reflect today's wage levels, Social Security adjusts, or 'indexes,' those earlier earnings. For example, if you earned $9,870 in 1978, it would be adjusted to $45,481 for someone retiring in 2024. This adjustment is done by comparing the average wage levels from the year you earned the income to the average wage levels near your retirement.[9]
- **A benefit that can continue to support your loved ones after you pass away.** Social Security provides crucial life and disability insurance benefits, with 70.6 million Americans relying on these programs in 2022 alone. According to the Center on Budget and Policy Priorities, for a younger worker with a spouse and two children, these benefits are equivalent to a life insurance policy with a face value of nearly $700,000, though the exact amount varies based on the worker's earnings history.[10]
- **You should feel confident that the benefits you'll receive from Social Security and Medicare often exceed the amount you paid in taxes over your lifetime.** For single men and women, as well as married couples across various wage

9 Social Security Administration, National Average Wage Index for 2022, available at SSA AWI https://www.ssa.gov/oact/cola/AWI.html

10 Social Security Administration, Fast Facts & Figures About Social Security, 2023, available at SSA Fast Facts 2023

levels, the total dollar value of benefits received from these programs typically surpasses the taxes paid into the system.[11]

WHO QUALIFIES FOR SOCIAL SECURITY?

If you're wondering whether or not you or your spouse qualify for retirement benefits, let's explore eligibility criteria:

1. **American workers**: The retired worker benefit is the main benefit that people think of when they hear the words Social Security. In order to qualify for your retired worker benefit, you need to earn at least 40 work credits over your lifetime. These credits are based on your earnings. In 2025, every $1,810 you earn equates to one credit, and every year a worker can earn up to four credits.

If you're the kind of person who can do math in your head, you might be thinking, great! I'll just work for 10 years, get my 40 credits and then sleep or party or do whatever before I retire! Sure, you could get what I think of as a Rip Van Winkle benefit: You would qualify even if you want to sleep your life away. But keep in mind that your benefit is based on your 35 years of *highest* indexed earnings. For every year shy of 35 that you don't work, the Social Security calculators will give you a big fat 0 in the formula. Because your benefit amount is based on what you earn, it's really not in your best interest to pull a Rip Van Winkle.

However, that doesn't mean you can't have a little fun. Want to vacation for 11 months of the year and still be eligible for Social Security? The most credits a person can earn per year are four, and in 2025, each $1,810 you earn qualifies you for one work credit. It stands to reason that if you can earn $7,240 (four credits' worth) in one month, then you can vacation the other 11 months of the year and still be eligible for a benefit.

11 Urban Institute, 'Social Security and Medicare Lifetime Benefits and Taxes,' July 2023

2. **Primary caretakers**: Another thing to mention is that even if you haven't held a job or worked under the Social Security platform, you might still qualify for spousal benefits. As a nonworking spouse, you may qualify to receive benefits and Medicare at age 65 even if you haven't earned 40 work credits if you meet the following criteria:
    - You are at least 62 years of age
    - You have been married for at least 12 months
    - Your spouse is currently receiving retirement or disability benefits.

You may still be eligible for spousal benefits even if you are divorced. The amount of your spousal benefits can be up to half as much as what your current or former partner would receive or is receiving for their full retirement amount. For example, if your ex-spouse is currently receiving $2,000 a month for their retired worker benefit, you may be eligible for 50% of that amount, or $1,000 a month, as long as that amount is lower than your own benefit, if you have one. Claiming this benefit does NOT reduce your spouse's or ex-spouse's benefit.

There are two categories of divorced spouses to consider:

1. **Divorced for less than 2 years**: Your ex-spouse must already be receiving Social Security retirement or disability benefits in order for you to claim a divorced spouse benefit.

2. **Divorced for 2 years or longer**: You and your ex-spouse must both be at least 62 years old. In this case, your divorced spouse benefit is based on your ex-spouse's full retirement age (FRA) benefit, regardless of what they are currently receiving.

UNDERSTANDING THE IMPACT OF THE SOCIAL SECURITY FAIRNESS ACT OF 2023 ON PUBLIC SECTOR EMPLOYEES

While most people are covered by Social Security, if you are also expecting to receive pension income, then your Social Security benefits could be lower. This is due to the Windfall Elimination Provision and the Government Pension Offset rules. Whether or not these rules will affect you depends on whether your pension is from private-sector or public-sector employment.

If your pension is from the private sector—such as a company or individual rather than the government—then your Social Security benefit will not be affected. Your Social Security payroll taxes have been funding the Social Security program.

If your pension is from the public-sector—such as a government agency, where you worked as a teacher, librarian or police officer, for example— then your payroll taxes may not be funding Social Security. If your pension comes from work where you did not pay Social Security taxes (common in some government jobs), the Windfall Elimination Provision (WEP) and Government Pension Offset (GPO) may reduce your Social Security benefits. These rules are designed to prevent 'double-dipping' by reducing Social Security benefits to account for pension income from non-covered employment.

While most people are covered by Social Security, if you are also expecting to receive pension income from public sector employment, there have been significant changes that could affect your benefits. The Social Security Fairness Act of 2023, signed into law on January 5, 2025, brings welcome changes for public sector workers.

Understanding Public vs Private Sector Pensions: If your pension is from the private sector—such as a company or individual rather than the government—your Social Security benefit has never been affected, as your Social Security payroll taxes have been funding the Social Security program.

However, if your pension is from the public sector—such as a government agency where you worked as a teacher, librarian, or police officer—historically your benefits may have been reduced under provisions known as WEP (Windfall Elimination Provision) and GPO (Government Pension Offset). These provisions were designed to prevent 'double-dipping' by reducing Social Security benefits for those receiving pension income from non-covered employment.

IMPORTANT UPDATE: The Social Security Fairness Act of 2023 Changes Everything

The passage of this landmark legislation eliminates both WEP and GPO, benefiting nearly 3 million public sector retirees. This means:

- Public sector workers will no longer face reductions in their Social Security benefits due to their government pensions
- Affected beneficiaries could see an average increase of $7,300 annually in their Social Security benefits.[12]
- The changes will apply to all benefits disbursed after December 2023

This represents a significant victory for public service workers, including:

- Teachers
- Firefighters
- Police officers
- Federal, state, and local government employees

---

12 Serving Those Who Serve – https://stwserve.com/the-social-security-fairness-act-key-points-for-csrs-employees/)

TIMING AND IMPLEMENTATION

If you're a public sector worker or retiree affected by WEP or GPO, you should see changes in your benefits soon after the law takes effect. Current retirees affected by these provisions will see immediate increases in their monthly Social Security payments.

This can also affect your claiming strategy if you've worked in both public and private sectors during your career. While the elimination of these provisions is generally positive for affected workers, it's still important to be intentional about when you file for benefits. There may be planning opportunities to optimize your Social Security benefits based on your unique work history and situation.

Note: For the most current information about how these changes might affect your specific situation, visit SocialSecurityClarity.com/resources to sign up for updates and receive the latest Social Security news as it happens.

IMPACT ON REAL-WORLD SCENARIOS

Let's look at how these changes affect public sector workers through two practical examples:

- **Example 1 -** Mixed Career Service: John worked for 25 years as a police officer in a public-sector job where he didn't pay Social Security taxes, but he also worked for 10 years in private-sector jobs where he did pay Social Security taxes. Under the old system, John's Social Security benefit would have been reduced from $1,200 to $800 per month due to WEP. With the passage of the Social Security Fairness Act, John will now receive his full $1,200 monthly Social Security benefit in addition to his police pension. This means an extra $400 per month, or $4,800 per year, in retirement income.

- **Example 2 -** Survivor Benefits: Sarah is a retired teacher with a government pension of $2,400 per month from a job where she didn't pay Social Security taxes. She is also eligible for a survivor benefit based on her deceased husband's Social Security record of $1,200 per month. Previously, under GPO, Sarah's survivor benefit would have been completely eliminated due to her teacher's pension. Under the new law, Sarah will receive her full survivor benefit of $1,200 per month in addition to her teacher's pension. This represents an increase in annual income of $14,400.

PLANNING OPPORTUNITIES These changes create new opportunities for public sector workers to maximize their retirement benefits:

1. If you previously opted not to work enough quarters to qualify for Social Security due to GPO/WEP concerns, you might want to reconsider working enough quarters to qualify for benefits.
2. If you're currently working in both public and private sectors, you no longer need to worry about penalties for "double-dipping" - your benefits from both systems will be honored fully.
3. If you're already retired and affected by WEP or GPO, you should see an automatic adjustment to your benefits after the law takes effect.

TAKING ACTION If you're a public sector worker or retiree, here are your next steps:

1. Review your Social Security statement to understand your potential benefit amount without WEP/GPO reductions.
2. Consider how this additional income might affect your overall retirement plan and tax situation.
3. If you haven't yet filed for Social Security benefits, review your claiming strategy in light of these changes.

4. If you're currently receiving reduced benefits due to WEP or GPO, watch for communications from the Social Security Administration about adjustments to your payments.

Remember, while these changes are overwhelmingly positive for public sector workers, the timing of when you claim your Social Security benefits remains an important decision that should be made as part of your overall retirement strategy. Consider working with a qualified financial advisor who can help you optimize your benefits under these new rules.

Note: For updates on implementation timelines and specific details about how these changes affect your situation, visit SocialSecurityClarity.com/resources.

WHEN DO YOU GET PAID?

When you're ready to begin receiving your Social Security benefit, or when you reach your full retirement age, the Social Security Administration isn't going to call you up and say, "Congratulations! It's time to collect your benefit!" You have to remember to file an application, and you also have to time your filing correctly so that your income arrives when you want it to.

You may file for your benefit in one of three ways:

1) **File for your benefit online (www.ssa.gov/retirement)**

2) **Call 1-800-772-1213** (TTY 1-800-325-0778)

3) Visit your **local Social Security office**. An appointment may not be required, but if you call ahead and schedule one, it may reduce the time you spend waiting to apply.

Social Security payment dates are based on your birthday. That makes it easy to remember when to expect your check to arrive!

- If your birthday is between the first and the 10th of the month, then you will receive your check on the second Wednesday of the month.
- If your birthday is between the 11th and 20th of the month, then you will receive your check on the third Wednesday of the month.
- If your birthday is between the 21st to the end of the month, then you will receive your check on the fourth Wednesday of the month.

WHEN IS YOUR FULL RETIREMENT AGE?

Full retirement age, sometimes referred to as FRA, is the age when you become entitled to receive full and unreduced retirement benefits. Back in the 1930s, full retirement age was 65 for everybody, but as we mentioned earlier, people today are living much longer than they did back then. Because of that, the 1983 amendments to Social Security phased in a gradual increase in FRA over a 22-year period. During this period, full retirement age will go from age 65 to 67.

What hasn't changed is the earliest age you can begin receiving benefits—that remains age 62.

As of 2025, if you were born in 1960 or later, then your full retirement age is 67. For those who are born before 1960, refer to this handy chart to locate your full retirement age:

THE FULL FRA BREAKDOWN

Birth Year	Full Retirement Age
1943–1954	66
1955	66 & 2 months
1956	66 & 4 months
1957	66 & 6 months

Birth Year	Full Retirement Age
1958	66 & 8 months
1959	66 & 10 months
1960 & later	67

Source: SSA

RECAP & WHAT'S NEXT

In this chapter, we clarified the basics of Social Security—who qualifies, what it is, and when you can access your benefits. Understanding these fundamentals is crucial for making informed decisions about your retirement.

To help you protect your Social Security number and Benefits from theft and fraudulent claims, please review and complete the **Social Security Fraud Defense Checklist™** provided at the end of this chapter.

The repeal of WEP and GPO marks a significant change in Social Security benefits, particularly for public-sector retirees. Stay informed about how these changes may benefit you by visiting SocialSecurityClarity.com/resources.

Next, we'll delve into the crucial question of how much you will actually receive, exploring the factors that influence your benefit amount and how to maximize it.

SOCIAL SECURITY FRAUD DEFENSE CHECKLIST™

STEPS TO PROTECT YOUR SOCIAL SECURITY BENEFIT FROM THEFT AND FRAUDULENT CLAIMS

Data breaches and cybersecurity threats have surged since the mid-2000s, with a record 234 million people affected by data breaches in 2023 alone.[13] Your Social Security number is your ticket to a lifetime income stream and is perhaps the single most important piece of government-issued documentation that an American citizen can own.

Before moving on, take a moment to protect the benefits you've earned. Below, you'll find the **Social Security Fraud Defense Checklist™**. This tool is designed to help you safeguard your Social Security number and benefits against theft and fraudulent claims. Completing this checklist can help prevent the loss of your benefits and ensure that your Social Security account remains secure:

1. **Open a my Social Security account**. This is your gateway to many online services, but more than that, it eliminates the risk of someone else trying to create an account in your name if they happen to obtain your number.
2. **Add a second method of identification to your My Social Security account.** This will provide you with an additional layer of security. If you have already registered at my Social Security, take a minute now to log in and add a second method of identification.
3. **Do not make it a practice to routinely carry around your Social Security card** or number or any documents that display your number. Be cautious about sharing this number, especially with an unsolicited caller. There may be times when you are asked for your number, in which case you want to make sure you ask why

13 SOURCES: Cybersecurity Dive, 'Data Compromises Hit Record High in 2023'. https://www.cybersecuritydive.com/news/data-compromises-record-high/696745/

your number is needed, how it will be used and what will happen if you refuse to share it.

4. **If you suspect identify theft, report it** to the Office of the Inspector General at **www.identitytheft.gov**. You can also block electronic access and any automated telephone access if you know your information has been compromised. When you use the Block Electronic Access feature, no one—including you!—can see or change your personal information over the internet. You may also reverse this decision by contacting Social Security.

5. **Monitor Your Credit Report Regularly**: Regularly checking your credit report can help you detect unauthorized activity that might indicate identity theft, such as new accounts opened in your name. You're entitled to a free credit report annually from each of the three major credit bureaus (Equifax, Experian, and TransUnion) through AnnualCreditReport.com.

6. **Consider Third-Party Identity Monitoring Services**: Third-party services like LifeLock, IdentityForce, or Experian IdentityWorks offer additional layers of protection. These services monitor your personal information across the web and alert you to any suspicious activity. They can also assist in the event of identity theft by helping to restore your identity and recover stolen funds.

7. **Set Up Account Alerts**: Enable notifications and alerts for your bank accounts, credit cards, and any financial accounts. Many institutions offer text or email alerts for suspicious activity, unusual logins, or large transactions. This can help you respond quickly if your Social Security number is being misused.

8. **Freeze Your Credit**: If you're not planning to apply for new credit, consider freezing your credit report with the three major credit bureaus. A credit freeze prevents lenders from accessing your credit report, making it harder for identity thieves to open accounts in your name.

For more tools and resources to help you navigate the complexities of Social Security, including a downloadable version of the Social Security Fraud Defense Checklist™, visit SocialSecurityClarity.com/resources.

CHAPTER 7

HOW MUCH WILL YOU GET?

"The art of being wise is the art of knowing what to overlook."
– WILLIAM JAMES

According to the Nationwide Retirement Institute® Consumer Social Security Report, **retirees are more likely to *overestimate* their benefit than they are to underestimate it**. In addition to this mistake, the trend has also been to claim as early as possible. How much will your monthly benefit be?

Consider these facts:

- In 2023, a third of insured workers claimed Social Security benefits as soon as they became eligible at the age of 62 .[14]
- Claiming early, before your full retirement age of 67, reduces your benefit amount by up to 24% .[15]

---

14 Social Security: Age Reduction," Social Security Administration, accessed SSA Age Reduction. https://www.ssa.gov/benefits/retirement/planner/agereduction.html

15 What Happens If I Collect Social Security Early?" Social Security Administration FAQ, accessed SSA FAQ. https://faq.ssa.gov/en-us/Topic/article/KA-01885

- Conversely, waiting to file until age 70 can increase your benefit by up to 32% .[16]

GET A SNEAK PEEK AT YOUR BENEFIT BEFORE YOU RETIRE

The Social Security Administration (SSA) no longer routinely mails out annual benefit statements to most workers. This change, implemented in 2011 as a cost-saving measure, means that paper statements are generally only sent to individuals aged 60 and over who are not receiving benefits and do not have an online account.

To access your statement, most workers need to create an online "my Social Security" account, where you can view, print, save, or request a mailed replacement statement at any time.

Fast Fact: Once you turn 60, you will start receiving a benefit statement every year if you haven't registered online and aren't already receiving benefits. If you have an online account, you can log in anytime to find out your expected benefits at different ages, including your primary insurance amount at full retirement age.[17]

HOW TO DECIPHER YOUR ESTIMATED BENEFITS

When discussing Social Security, you may have encountered a variety of acronyms that can make understanding your benefits a bit confusing. We've already touched on SSA (Social Security Administration) and FRA (full retirement age). Other key acronyms include FRA and PIA, which are essential to understanding your benefits.

16 Raising Social Security's Retirement Age Would Cut Benefits for All New Retirees," Center on Budget and Policy Priorities, accessed CBPP Retirement Age. https://www.cbpp.org/research/social-security/raising-social-securitys-retirement-age-would-cut-benefits-for-all-new

17 POMS: RS 01404.100 - Social Security Statement Process." Social Security Administration. Available at:https://secure.ssa.gov/poms.nsf/lnx/0205002005

FRA (Full Retirement Age): For people born before 1937, the FRA was 65. It gradually increased for those born between 1938 and 1942. For individuals born between 1943 and 1954, the FRA is 66. It then increases by two-month intervals for each birth year until it reaches 67 for those born in 1960 or later. Therefore, the FRA is 67 for anyone born in 1960 or later.

PIA (Primary Insurance Amount): This is the amount of your monthly Social Security benefit if you start receiving benefits at your full retirement age. It is calculated based on your highest 35 years of indexed earnings and is rounded down to the nearest whole dollar. If you start receiving benefits at your FRA, your benefit is neither reduced for early retirement nor increased for delayed retirement credits.

Your PIA is determined using a formula that considers several factors, including:

- **How long you worked**
- **How much you earned each year** (with adjustments for inflation)
- **The rate of inflation** (which affects how your earnings are indexed)

HOW MUCH WILL YOU GET?

How much money you will get from your benefit depends on when you file. It's not just the year that matters; the month also factors into the equation. Between ages 62 and 70, there are 96 months you could file, and each month would result in a different benefit amount.

If you claim *before* your full retirement age (or FRA), Social Security will assess a penalty or actuarial reduction. For example, if your primary insurance amount (PIA) is $2,000 at your FRA of 67, here's how the reduction applies for earlier filing:

- **Age 62:** $1,400
- **Age 63:** $1,500

- **Age 64:** $1,600
- **Age 65:** $1,733
- **Age 66:** $1,867
- **Age 67:** $2,000

Conversely, if you claim *after* your full retirement age, the SSA rewards you with a prize called delayed retirement credits. Every month past your full retirement age that you wait to claim will increase or grow that benefit amount. This growth or increase is represented by a percentage amount, based on the month of your birth. Once you reach age 70, the benefit is said to be fully ripe—like a piece of fruit — and waiting any longer to "pick" or claim your benefit is no longer to your advantage.

Using our same example of a $2,000 PIA at a full retirement age of 67, here's how delaying your claim can increase your benefit:

- **Age 68:** $2,160
- **Age 69:** $2,320
- **Age 70:** $2,480

Fast Fact: There is no additional benefit gained if you wait past the age of 70 to file for your benefit.

HOW DO YOU DECIDE: NOW OR LATER?

While $2,480 sure sounds better than $1,400 you have to remember that most people don't receive any income from Social Security while waiting for their benefit to grow to a larger starting point.

At the end of the day, deciding when to file is not just based on the amount of income you want to receive. Other considerations such as your health and the needs of your spouse factor into the equation.

There is also the impact of longevity and having a larger inflation adjusted, often lower taxed, source income.

There are many good reasons for filing early and good reasons for filing late, but filing just because you don't know what else to do is probably not one of them.

Bonus Content Alert: Visit SocialSecurityClarity.com/resources to find videos that explain the pros and cons of both early and delayed claiming.

Most people when deciding think only about their break-even point. This concept is popular because it simplifies the decision process, but it may not give you the full picture. The break-even calculation factors in the number of years you would receive additional income if you filed early versus the years of missing income followed by the years of extra income you would receive if you filed late. Comparing the two scenarios may tell you when you break even, or when the amount of money you earn will be the same.

A very basic break-even analysis shows that someone claiming at age 62 would receive close to $375,000 in lifetime income dollars by around age 78, which is also when they would receive that same amount had they waited and filed at age 70. However, this analysis shows you only the benefits inside of a vacuum. It doesn't consider the impact on your investment accounts, taxes, the surviving spouse's benefit, and it doesn't consider the biggest threat to your retirement success: longevity.

PLAYING SOCIAL SECURITY ROULETTE: WHAT ARE YOUR ODDS?

There is one perfect month between the ages of 62 and 70 that is the best month to apply for your benefits. That's an eight-year time period of 96 months. One of those 96 months represents the very best decision that you could possibly make, the decision that would give you the highest paychecks for the longest period of time.

The only problem is that in order to get that month just exactly right, you have to know exactly when you will die.

Of course, no one has a crystal ball. You can get hung up on this and play what I call Social Security roulette: Step right up and spin the wheel! You'll have a 96-1 chance that the marble will drop in just the right slot, and you'll get this decision right.

Or . . .

You can consider your family and health history and use a life expectancy calculator. You can work with a knowledgeable advisor and be equipped with all of the information you need to make a good decision on the filing strategy that can help ensure you stack the odds for a successful outcome.

Fast Fact: According to recent surveys conducted by the Pew Research Center, the median desired life span in America is approximately 89 years.[18]

---

18 Pew Research Center, "Number of People 100 and Older is Growing in the U.S. and Around the World," January 9, 2023. Available at: https://www.pewresearch.org/fact-tank/2023/01/09/number-of-people-100-and-older-is-growing-in-us-and-around-the-world/.

LIVING LONGER AND INCREASING LIFETIME INCOME

We talked earlier about how longevity magnifies all other risks. Well, here's a bit of good news: **When it comes to claiming your Social Security benefit, longevity magnifies your income!** The longer you wait to file and the longer you live, the more you stand to gain in terms of your benefits.

Take a look at these numbers using that same illustration of a break-even concept, imagining someone who lives until age 90:

- **If they file at age 62,** they receive a total of about **$622,460** in lifetime income.
- **If they file at age 67 (FRA),** they receive a total of about **$692,279** in lifetime income.
- **If they file at age 70,** they receive a total of about **$723,090** in lifetime income.

If you knew that your Social Security benefit was an investment portfolio worth over $700,000, how would that change how you think about this benefit? The potential is there, yet most people don't look at it that way. The longer you live, the higher your total lifetime distribution will be.

Here is another hypothetical illustration assuming a 2% inflationary factor for COLA adjustments and that same $2,000 benefit at FRA:

If you live until age 72:

- Your total income amount if you file early at age 62 will be $183,955
- Your total income amount if you file later at age 70 will be $60,115.

✓ Claiming *early* will give you a $123,840 higher lifetime income.

If you live until age 85:

- Your total income amount if you file early at age 62 will be $484,595.
- Your total income amount if you file later at age 70 will be $858,426.

✓ Claiming *later* will give you a $373,831 higher lifetime income.

If you live until age 90:

- Your total income amount if you file early at age 62 will be $622,460.
- Your total income amount if you file later at age 70 will be 1,102,644.

✓ Claiming *later* will give you a $480,184 higher lifetime income. (Wow!)

As you can see, the longer you live, the more you stand to gain by delaying your claiming strategy. However, as we said earlier, the numbers aren't the only thing you have to consider. There are other factors such as your health and your spouse, and there are also filing options available that you might not even know about.

RECAP & WHAT'S NEXT

In this chapter, we discussed how much you can expect to receive from Social Security and the factors that influence your benefit amount. We explored the impact of filing early versus delaying your claim, how your benefit is calculated based on your highest earning years, and the significance of understanding your PIA and FRA. The key takeaway is that your filing decision is crucial and can significantly impact your lifetime income.

To help you visualize how different filing decisions might impact your total lifetime benefits, don't forget to use the **Future Income Assessment Worksheet™** provided at the end of this chapter. This exercise will offer you a clearer picture of the financial implications of your choices.

Looking ahead, knowing how much you will receive from Social Security is critical, but there's another important factor to consider: *the future of the Social Security system itself.* With concerns about potential benefit cuts and the system's long-term solvency, it's natural to wonder if your benefits will be there when you need them. In the next chapter, we'll explore these issues and help you understand what you can do to protect your financial future.

FUTURE INCOME ASSESSMENT WORKSHEET™

Did you know? The average retiree leaves $111,000 in lifetime benefits unclaimed due to suboptimal timing. Before you make any decisions, it's essential to understand the financial implications of different claiming ages. The **Future Income Assessment Worksheet™** is designed to help you calculate your potential lifetime Social Security income based on various filing ages. This exercise will give you a clearer picture of how much you stand to gain or lose, depending on when you choose to file.

INSTRUCTIONS:

1. Fill in your estimated monthly and annual benefits at ages 62 and 70, as provided in your Social Security benefits statement.
2. Use these numbers to project your total lifetime income based on different life expectancy scenarios.
3. If you're married, complete the same exercise for your spouse to understand the combined impact on your household income.

How much income will you receive at age 62?

Per month: ____________________ Per Year: ____________________

How much income will you receive at age 70?

Per month: ____________________ Per Year: ____________________

Now multiply that yearly amount based on the following terms:

Filing at age 62 and living until age 75 (yearly income X 13)______
Filing at age 70 and living until age 75 (yearly income X 5)_______
Filing at age 62 and living until age 85 (yearly income X 23)______
Filing at age 70 and living until age 85 (yearly income X 15)______
Filing at age 62 and living until age 90 (yearly income X 28)______

Filing at age 70 and living until age 90 (yearly income X 20)_____

If you are married, also take the time to fill out these numbers for your spouse:

How much income will your spouse receive at age 62?

Per month: __________________ Per Year: ________________

How much income will your spouse receive at age 70?

Per month: __________________ Per Year: ________________

Now multiply that yearly amount based on the following terms:

Filing at age 62 and living until age 75 (yearly income X 13)_____
Filing at age 70 and living until age 75 (yearly income X 5)______
Filing at age 62 and living until age 85 (yearly income X 23)_____
Filing at age 70 and living until age 85 (yearly income X 15)_____
Filing at age 62 and living until age 90 (yearly income X 28)_____
Filing at age 70 and living until age 90 (yearly income X 20)_____

For a downloadable PDF of the **Future Income Assessment Worksheet™** and additional resources to help you navigate your Social Security decisions, visit SocialSecurityClarity.com/resources.

CHAPTER 8

WILL SOCIAL SECURITY COLLAPSE?

Alarmists who claim that Social Security won't be around when today's young workers retire either misunderstand or misrepresent the projections.
—CENTER ON BUDGET AND POLICY PRIORITIES

It used to be that Social Security was a solid leg of the retirement stool—a concept that includes three legs to support retirement income, pensions, Social Security, and personal savings. Today, pensions are few and far between, and the Social Security system is facing similar solvency concerns. The pressure on individuals has never been greater, and people are afraid. They want to know, "Will the system be there to support us when we need it? Are there benefit cuts in our future? Should we file early and get it now while we can?"

As of 2024, if policymakers take no further action, Social Security can only afford to pay 77% of scheduled benefits starting in 2033.[19] That's less than one decade away as of the writing of this book! If

19 Social Security Administration. "Projections of Social Security Trust Fund Depletion." Presentation by the Office of the Chief Actuary, November 15, 2023. Accessed August 2024. https://www.ssa.gov/oact/presentations/ocact_20231115.pdf

you're nearing retirement while reading this book, you might be thinking about the long-term game of retirement and wondering, if I wait to file, will it pay off? Will it be worth it to wait and give up those first years of receiving early income if later benefits will receive a cut? Or is it even more advantageous to wait given your future benefits may be reduced by a certain percentage amount?

I wrote this chapter to answer just such concerns. My goal is to give you not just my opinion, but some facts. Of all the reasons to file without a strategy, fear is perhaps the most destructive to your plan.

I believe that Social Security will evolve because the system needs to change in order to continue at its current pace. It's not failing because it's a bad system; it's failing because it's being asked to do something it wasn't designed to do. But you don't have to take my word for it. Let's talk about why the system is in trouble, how policy changes in the past have helped and what possible future changes may affect you.

3 REASONS WHY THE SYSTEM ISN'T ABLE TO KEEP UP

#1: INCREASES IN LIFE EXPECTANCY RATES WITHOUT A COMPARABLE INCREASE IN THE RETIREMENT AGE

OK, so reason No. 1 isn't really a big surprise. The system is in trouble because we've been living longer, yet we still want to retire at age 62. (Who can blame us? We're only human, after all.) We talked earlier about how much longer people are living and how much pressure those extra years of living can put on a retirement portfolio. The Social Security system is also feeling the same pressure. Consider these facts:

- When Social Security began paying out benefits in 1937, the average 65-year-old male could expect to live another 11.9 years to age 76.9. By 2024, that number increased by 6.2 years to age 83.1, while the retirement age has only increased by one and half years. That's a 47% increase in the time spent collecting benefits.

- For the average 65-year-old female, the time of retirement increased by 7.9 years between 1940 and 2024, from 78.4 in 1940 to 86.3 in 2024, yet again the retirement age has only increased by a year and a half. That's a 49% increase in the time spent collecting benefits.
- Your Social Security benefit is automatically indexed every year to keep up with inflation, yet the retirement age is not automatically indexed to keep up with the increased life expectancy rates.[20]

Changes that were made: In 1983, changes were made to gradually increase the retirement age from 65 to age 67. This change is still being phased in, yet it's been over 35 years since the amendments passed.[21]

Any future changes to the full retirement age will also likely be done over a period of time.

#2: INCREASE IN THE NUMBER OF BENEFICIARIES DUE TO THE NUMBER OF PEOPLE BORN DURING THE BABY BOOMER GENERATION

If you're interested in Social Security, then there's a pretty good chance you might be a member of the boomer generation, born between the years of 1946 and 1964.[22] During that time, the average birth rate reached an all-time high of 3.7 children per woman.[23] In contrast, by 2023, the birth rate had dropped to about 1.6, the lowest rate on

20 US Life Expectancy 1950 - 2024 – MacroTrends https://www.macrotrends.net/global-metrics/countries/USA/united-states/life-expectancy

21 Social Security Administration (SSA). "The 1983 Amendments." https://www.ssa.gov/policy/docs/ssb/v66n1/v66n1p1.html

22 Social Security Administration (SSA). "2023 Trustees Report." Available at: https://www.ssa.gov/OACT/TR/2023/tr2023.pdf

23 Pew Research Center. "Baby Boomers Retire." Available at: https://www.pewresearch.org/fact-tank/2023/01/13/baby-boomers-retire/

record. The Social Security system is stressed because today, we're seeing those boomers reach full retirement age in waves.

Fast Fact: Between the years of 2011 and 2032, it is projected that the number of people eligible for their retirement benefits will increase by 65% while the number of people paying into the system will increase by a comparable 18%.

Changes that were made: In 2015, Congress passed the Bipartisan Budget Act to close two unintended loopholes to the system that allowed some married couples and families to increase their benefits.[24] By closing these loopholes, payments of full disability benefits into 2022 were ensured and the proposed increases to Medicare Part B premiums were reduced, among other things.

#3: CHANGING TRENDS IN DISABILITY BENEFITS

In the past, the number of people receiving disability benefits increased significantly, contributing to the strain on the Social Security system.[25] However, recent trends show that the number of disability beneficiaries has been declining since its peak in 2014.[26] As of 2023, the average monthly disability benefit was about $1,483.[27] The 2023 Social Security Trustees' Report projects that the Disability Insurance (DI) Trust Fund will remain solvent until 2057, longer than previously anticipated, due to lower-than-expected applications and awards of disability benefits. [28] This decline reflects demographic and economic changes that have eased pressures on the program, suggesting that

24 Congressional Research Service. "Bipartisan Budget Act of 2015." Available at: https://crsreports.congress.gov/product/pdf/IN/IN10334
25 Social Security Administration (SSA). "2023 Trustees Report." Available at: https://www.ssa.gov/OACT/TR/2023/tr2023.pdf
26 Ibid.
27 Social Security Administration. "Monthly Statistical Snapshot, June 2023." Available at: https://www.ssa.gov/policy/docs/quickfacts/stat_snapshot/
28 Social Security Administration (SSA). "2023 Trustees Report." Available at: https://www.ssa.gov/OACT/TR/2023/tr2023.pdf

the share of Americans receiving disability insurance will remain stable in the coming decades.[29]

When Social Security was created, the system worked effectively, but the needs and conditions of today's population require adjustments to ensure its sustainability. These adjustments are necessary, especially for those nearing retirement, to ensure the system remains robust and reliable.

WHO MOVED MY SOCIAL SECURITY?

Change can be a scary thing. Fear of change can also build up and compound (like interest) in your mind. But is the fear of what you imagine ever as bad as the situation that actually exists? Spencer Johnson, the author of the best-selling book *Who Moved My Cheese?*, says that it is not. "When you stop being afraid, you feel good," he writes. "The quicker you let go of old cheese, the sooner you find the new cheese."

He also advocates for a sense of humor. To continue his metaphor, if your old cheese is fear, then it's probably filled with holes because of what you don't know. So, consider this chapter your new piece of cheese. Let's take a minute to fill in those holes.

Changes to the Social Security system have been happening since the system was first introduced into law, and those changes were made in the name of good. They provide comprehensive protection for American workers and their families against the loss of earnings. One analysis by the Center on Budget and Policy Priorities estimates that Social Security lifts more than 22 million Americans out of poverty, and more than 15 million of those people were over the age of 65.[30]

29 Center on Budget and Policy Priorities. "Disability Insurance in the United States." Available at: https://www.cbpp.org/research/social-security/disability-insurance-in-the-united-states

30 Center on Budget and Policy Priorities. "Policy Basics: Top Ten Facts about Social Security." Available at: https://www.cbpp.org/research/social-security/policy-basics-top-ten-facts-about-social-security

If the Social Security system is to survive, it needs to change, and it's helpful to remember that the system has changed before. The list of amendments that have been passed to the Old Age, Survivors and Disability Insurance Program (OASDI)—what the federal government refers to as Social Security—could easily fill its own book. (And these are only the major changes; there have also been less significant amendments passed, which, if you're really curious, can be found by checking out the Congressional Research Service.)

But have we ever been in this much trouble before?

Between 1977 and 1983, our nation experienced a period of spiraling inflation, high unemployment and worse-than-expected economic conditions that utterly drained Social Security. Things were looking so bad that trust fund analysts reported that Social Security "would be unable to pay benefits on time by some point in the 1980s.[31]" The amendments signed into law in 1983 by President Reagan gave a renewed promise to the American people:

> Our elderly need no longer fear that the checks they depend on will be stopped or reduced. These amendments protect them. Americans of middle age need no longer worry whether their career-long investment will pay off. These amendments guarantee it. And younger people can feel confident that Social Security will still be around when they need it to cushion their retirement.
>
> **— PRESIDENT REAGAN, DURING THE SIGNING OF THE SOCIAL SECURITY AMENDMENTS OF 1983[32]**

These changes were designed to solve the short-range financing problem and reduce by two-thirds the projected deficit. They accomplished those goals in part with the gradual increase in the

31 Social Security Administration (SSA). "The 1983 Amendments: How the Last Major Social Security Reforms Came About." Available at: https://www.ssa.gov/history/1983amend.html

32 Ibid.

age of eligibility for full retirement benefits from age 65 to age 66 by 2009 and age 67 by 2027.[33] Additional provisions limited "windfall" benefits for certain workers who were already receiving government benefits, either for themselves or their spouses.

But most importantly, these changes worked. In the past, Social Security has collected more in taxes and other income than it has paid out in benefits and the system has amassed combined trust funds of $2.8 trillion, invested in interest-bearing Treasury securities.[34]

However, in recent years, Social Security has been paying out more in benefits than it is taking in through taxes and other income. The system is now operating at a deficit, with the trust funds being drawn down to cover the shortfall

WHAT NOW?

Today, we're faced with another projected shortfall. In 2015, the Bipartisan Budget Act was passed to close up two unintended loopholes in order to save an estimated $168 billion over the next 75-year planning horizon. Overall, the changes were relatively minor. They affect married couples and the amount they are able to claim on a spousal benefit. The changes were made to preserve the fairness of the incentives to delay filing.

From 2015:

According to estimates from Social Security's Chief Actuary, the changes would improve long-term solvency of the combined OASDI trust fund by 0.04 percent of payroll over 75 years.

33 Social Security Administration (SSA). "Retirement Benefits." Available at: https://www.ssa.gov/pubs/EN-05-10035.pdf
34 Social Security Administration (SSA). "2023 Trustees Report." Available at: https://www.ssa.gov/OACT/TR/2023/tr2023.pdf

Over the next 10 years, the Chief Actuary estimates these changes will save the trust funds between $5 billion and $9 billion, and CBO estimates these changes will save about $3 billion.

This bill would close 1.5 percent of the 75-year shortfall and reduce total Social Security costs by about 0.1 percent.

Following are the two main changes that were made and how they may affect you.

CHANGE #1: *THE TIMING OF MORE THAN ONE BENEFIT (ALSO CALLED DEEMED FILING)*

How it used to be: If you were eligible for both a spousal benefit and your own benefit, you could claim your spousal benefit and receive a check equal to half of your spouse's PIA benefit while you waited for your own benefit to grow. Then you could stop receiving your spousal benefit, and switch over to your new, higher amount. This created a different level of flexibility and strategy when navigating benefits for married couples.

How it is now: The deemed filing rule says that you can no longer file *only* for your spousal benefit and delay filing for your own retirement. When you file for one type of benefit, you are filing for all your benefits and will be awarded what the SSA calls a combination of the two benefits that equals the higher amount. There are exceptions to this rule, and deemed filing does not apply to survivor benefits.

What you may not know: In the past, you may have been able to claim half of your spouse's benefit while waiting to file for your own benefit, if both spouses were at full retirement age or older. However, this claiming strategy is no longer available. The restricted application option, which allowed this type of coordinated filing, has been eliminated for individuals born after 1953. As a result, you can no longer use this approach to fill an income gap while waiting to claim your own maximum retirement benefit.

CHANGE #2: *THE VOLUNTARY SUSPENSION OF BENEFITS (ALSO CALLED FILE AND SUSPEND.)*

How it used to be: If you reached full retirement age, you could file and suspend your benefit so that your spouse could receive a spousal benefit even though you weren't yet receiving a benefit. This allowed one spouse to grow their benefit and file later, thereby receiving a higher benefit check. File and suspend was the legal paperwork you had to file in order to accomplish the strategy above.

How it is now: After the Bipartisan Budget Act of 2015, the rules changed. You can still file and suspend your benefits if you have reached your full retirement age and are younger than 70. However, under the new rules, if you suspend your benefits, no other benefits (such as spousal or dependent benefits) can be paid on your record during the suspension period. Additionally, you cannot receive benefits based on another person's record during the suspension period.

What you may not know: If you are a divorced spouse, you can continue receiving a divorced spousal benefit even if your ex-spouse voluntarily suspends his or her own retirement benefit. This new law applies to individuals who request a suspension on or after April 30, 2016. You must have reached your full retirement age in order to request a suspension.

THE GOLDEN AGE OF SOCIAL SECURITY?

The budget act did save the system billions of dollars, but in order to ensure that a *"career-long investment will pay off,"* more changes still need to be made. The good news is that it only requires relatively modest changes to fully fund the system, and these changes won't likely affect you if you are inside the window of retirement.

For one thing, it would be political suicide to take away a promised benefit. For another, if the last 83 years of amendments have taught us anything, it's that any change to the benefits that affect millions of American lives will likely take place gradually, over the course of many years.

Fast Fact: The long-term gap between Social Security's projected income and promised benefits is estimated at 1.3% of gross domestic product (GDP) over the next 75 years (and 1.5% of GDP in the 75th year).[35]

The changes that are likely to occur in order to create solvency will likely include gradually increasing full retirement age and increasing the earnings cap. The earnings cap is the amount of your income subject to Social Security tax, which will be capped at $176,100 for 2025 (an increase from $168,600 in 2024). Experts also predict a potential increase in the payroll tax rate in the future to address solvency concerns, although the current rate remains at 12.4% (6.20% for employees and employers each). None of these changes would have a negative impact on someone who is retired today, nor would they likely impact the benefits of someone currently near retirement as of the writing of this book.

35 https://www.cbpp.org/research/social-security/key-principles-for-strengthening-social-security

RECAP & WHAT'S NEXT

In this chapter, we addressed concerns about the future of Social Security and explored the factors contributing to the system's current challenges. While the future of Social Security may seem uncertain, understanding the reasons behind these issues can help you approach your retirement planning with greater confidence. Remember, informed decisions today can lead to better outcomes tomorrow.

To ensure you're maximizing your Social Security benefits and taking full advantage of the options available to you, take a moment to complete the **Household Benefits Optimizer™** worksheet provided at the end of this chapter. This tool will guide you through evaluating your eligibility for various filing strategies and help you identify areas where you might optimize your benefits. Understanding potential changes helps you make informed decisions. Use this tool to evaluate your eligibility and claiming strategy under different scenarios and help you identify areas where you might optimize your benefits.

In the next chapter, we'll shift our focus to specific strategies and actions you can take to secure your financial confidence, ensuring that your retirement plan is as resilient as possible in the face of potential changes.

HOUSEHOLD BENEFITS OPTIMIZER™

KNOW THE RULES THAT APPLY TO YOUR HOUSEHOLD:

UNDERSTAND HOW TO TAKE ADVANTAGE OF THE BENEFITS YOU ARE ENTITLED TO

In the words of Spencer Johnson, "It is safer to search the maze than to remain in a cheeseless situation." Take a moment to answer the following questions to see if you might be eligible for a filing strategy that could help you optimize your Social Security benefits.

1. **Are you currently married?**

   ☐ Yes ☐ No

   If you answered yes, continue. If you answered no, move on to question No. 4.

2. **Have you and your spouse considered how the income situation will change for the surviving spouse?**

   ☐ Yes ☐ No

3. **Have you and your spouse investigated whether or not you may be eligible for a 67/70 filing strategy that can allow you to receive additional funds to help you bridge the income gap while waiting for one benefit to grow?**

   ☐ Yes ☐ No

4. **Are you eligible for divorce or survivor benefits?**

   ☐ Yes ☐ No

5. **If you answered yes, have you investigated whether or not your divorce/survivor benefits are higher than your own benefits?**

   ☐ Yes ☐ No

6. **Do you know who to talk to about your filing strategy?**

   ☐ Yes ☐ No

7. **Do you feel confident that you have identified your "better way" when it comes to filing for your Social Security benefit?**

   ☐ Yes ☐ No

Based on your responses, you may have identified areas where you could optimize your Social Security benefits. Here's what your answers indicate:

- **If you answered Yes to most questions**: You are on the right track! Consider discussing your strategy with a financial advisor to fine-tune your approach or confirm that you're maximizing your benefits for your situation. You can also explore our online resources at SocialSecurityClarity.com/resources for further guidance.
- **If you answered No to any question**: You may have uncovered opportunities for improvement. It's crucial to explore these areas further to ensure you're not leaving money on the table. Speaking with a financial advisor can help you navigate the complexities and make the most informed decisions.

For a downloadable PDF of the **Household Benefits Optimizer™** and additional resources to keep you informed and help you navigate Social Security decisions, visit SocialSecurityClarity.com/resources.

STEP 2

EVALUATION

"If you don't measure it, you can't manage it."
– PETER DRUCKER

The Evaluation step is where you begin to connect the dots between your collected data and the potential Social Security claiming strategies available to you. Building on the groundwork laid in the Preparation step, this phase involves using software or social security optimization trained professionals to model how different claiming strategies could affect your benefits over time, tailored to your unique situation.

The objective of the Evaluation step is to lay out all the potential options on the table, making it clear which strategy will best maximize your Social Security benefits while aligning with your broader retirement goals. This step is crucial in helping you visualize the long-term implications of each approach, ensuring you make an informed decision.

KEY ACTIONS IN THE EVALUATION STEP:[36]

1. **Model Claiming Scenarios**: Utilize reputable analysis tools or services to simulate various Social Security claiming strategies, considering factors like age, income needs, health status, and retirement timelines.
2. **Analyze and Compare Outcomes**: Review the results from each scenario to understand the potential benefits and trade-offs associated with different claiming ages and strategies.
3. **Select the Optimal Strategy**: Based on the analysis, identify the strategy that offers the highest potential lifetime benefits and best fits your overall retirement planning goals.

This evaluation helps ensure you're well-prepared to choose a Social Security strategy that is best for you and your family.

Get your personalized Social Security Analysis at SocialSecurityClarity.com/analyze.

36 *Disclaimer: The Retirement Analysis gives estimates based on your actual Social Security earning record. Please keep in mind that these are just estimates. We can't provide your actual benefit amount until you apply for benefits. And that amount may be different from the estimates provided.*

CHAPTER 9

STOP LEAVING MONEY ON THE TABLE

Jane is eligible for a widow's benefit, but she is unsure about what she is entitled to and how the process works. At 60 years old, Jane is five years younger than her late husband, Jim, who passed away at age 65 without ever filing for his Social Security benefit. Jane knows that if Jim had filed at his full retirement age of 67, his benefit would have been $2,000 per month. She's also aware that the earliest she can file for her own benefit is at age 62, which would yield $1,200 per month based on her earnings.

Feeling financially strained after losing Jim's income, Jane knows she needs to act quickly, and filing for Social Security seems like the easiest solution. A well-meaning friend advises her to visit the Social Security Administration (SSA) office to file for her widow's benefit, something Jane didn't even know she was eligible for at age 60.

Upon visiting the SSA office, Jane learns she is indeed eligible for the widow's benefit. She completes the paperwork and, in the process, unknowingly files for her retirement benefit as well. This decision results in a monthly payment of $1,430 for the rest of her life.

Initially, Jane feels relieved about her decision—until she realizes she had other, more lucrative options. With the right strategy, she could *have received up to $2,000 per month, potentially leaving $99,000 in lifetime benefits on the table simply because she wasn't fully informed.*

UNDERSTANDING THE RULES THAT APPLY TO YOUR HOUSEHOLD

In addition to deciding when to file for your retired worker benefit, you must also consider other critical benefits such as spousal, divorced, and survivor benefits. These options are designed to provide essential income support for individuals at their most vulnerable moments. Additionally, these benefits can extend to family members, including children, a surviving spouse, and even dependent parents.

Fast Fact: Married couples have 81 different ways to claim Social Security, resulting in over 8,000 different combinations. Single individuals have variations on nine different scenarios.[37]

Whether you are single, married, or divorced, you have multiple options when it comes to filing for your Social Security benefits. This chapter will guide you through the three main claiming options available to married, divorced, and widowed individuals. At the end of this chapter, you'll see what Jane could have done to achieve a better outcome.

CLAIMING OPTIONS THAT EVERY PERSON SHOULD KNOW

The difference between the worst way to file and the best way could be the difference between hundreds of thousands of dollars in lifetime income. For married individuals, these decisions are even more critical because they can affect the lives of two people instead of one.

37 CNBC, "Social Security Puzzle: Married Couples Can Claim 8,000 Ways," May 31, 2015. Available at: https://www.cnbc.com/2015/05/31/social-security-puzzle-married-couples-can-claim-8000-ways.html

As a married, divorced or widowed individual filing for a benefit, you may do any of the following:

- File early
- File late
- File at FRA

- File on a spouse's record
- File on a divorced spouse's record
- File survivor benefits

These filing decisions can be combined and recombined in numerous different ways with your early/late decision to get thousands of different out-comes, especially when you consider the month and year of your filing.

Let's take a look at the three main options available to people who are married, divorced or widowed.

OPTION #1: SPOUSAL BENEFITS

Spousal benefits were designed to protect the individual who worked in partnership taking care of the home and raising children. This person may not have earned as much taxable income as his or her spouse, but they may be eligible to receive up to 50% of their spouse's PIA. (Remember, PIA is their primary insurance amount at full retirement age.)

One thing to note is that spousal benefits are payable when your spouse begins receiving their own retirement or disability benefits. There is no added benefit to waiting until your spouse reaches age 70 before you file for the spousal benefit.

To qualify for spousal benefits, you must meet these three requirements:

- Have been married at least one year
- Have a spouse who is currently receiving their retirement or disability benefits
- Have a PIA that is less than one-half the PIA of your spouse

It's up to the primary earner (with a higher PIA) in the household to realize that their filing decision will have the greatest impact on the spousal benefit. This is such a critical piece, we spent an entire chapter on how NOT to hurt your spouse. While filing early does reduce the spousal benefit for the lower-earning spouse, there is no added benefit to the higher-earning spouse waiting until age 70 to file.

As a married person with children, a spouse may also be entitled to family benefits. These can pay out to a surviving spouse and children even after the worker dies, even if they never got to retire and file for Social Security.

OPTION #2: DIVORCE BENEFITS

Even if you have been divorced for 30 years, if you haven't remarried, you may still be eligible to collect divorce benefits from your ex-spouse. Divorce benefits apply to both the ex-wife and the ex-husband, and they also apply to couples in a same-sex marriage. If you qualify, your new benefit check will be equal to half of your ex's full retirement age PIA. If your benefit is already higher than half of his or her PIA, then you'll receive benefits based on your own work record.

Fast Fact: In a 2024 survey by Fidelity, 52% of respondents believed that their Social Security benefits could be reduced if an ex-spouse made a claim. However, this is not true. Your benefits are calculated based on your own or your ex-spouse's earnings record, and their actions will not reduce the amount you receive.[38]

Your ex has no say whatsoever on whether or not you can file for divorce benefits. You don't have to get their permission because they will never know on whose work record your benefit is based. They may not prevent you from filing. Furthermore, your decision to claim divorce benefits will NOT reduce or affect the payout of your ex-spouse whatsoever.

38 Fidelity. "5 Social Security Myths Debunked." Fidelity Viewpoints, June 7, 2024. https://www.fidelity.com/viewpoints/retirement/social-security-myths.

In order to claim on your ex-spouse's work record, you must meet the following requirements:

- You and your ex-spouse must have been married for at least 10 consecutive years
- Both you and your ex-spouse must be at least age 62
- You must not be remarried
- If you've been divorced for less than 2 years, your ex must already be receiving retirement or disability benefits for you to claim a divorced spouse benefit.
- If you've been divorced for 2 years or longer, you and your ex-spouse only need to be at least age 62, regardless of whether they have filed for benefits.

If you've remarried, your benefits (spousal, divorce, or survivor) will be based on your current spouse's work record, even if your ex-spouse has a higher PIA. Once remarried, you lose eligibility to claim based on your ex-spouse's record.

OPTION #3: SURVIVOR BENEFITS

When one spouse passes away, not only will the surviving spouse lose his or her life partner, but they will also lose one Social Security check if you are both retired. The impact of this can be minimized through the use of a claiming strategy because the surviving spouse has choices.

Survivor benefits are sometimes called widow or widower benefits. As the survivor, you can choose to receive the larger of these three benefit amounts:

- Your own benefit check
- The benefit check of the deceased
- A reduced survivor benefit if you claim it early, as early as age 60 (or 50 if disabled), which may be smaller than the full survivor benefit but can be switched to your own benefit at a later date to maximize total income.

A widow or widower qualifies for this benefit once they reach age 60, but if they remarry before that time, they forfeit their benefits. If you wait until age 60 before getting remarried, then you may still collect your survivor benefit. This is sometimes referred to as a "marriage penalty," the complexities of which should be examined by a qualified professional.

The survivor benefit is based on two things:

1. When the deceased filed
2. When the survivor files

In 2023, Social Security benefits kept nearly 22 million Americans out of poverty, with more than 15 million of those being adults aged 65 or older.[39]

HOW TO GET SOCIAL SECURITY BENEFITS EVEN AFTER YOU'RE DEAD

Most people think of Social Security as a benefit that ends once you stop fogging up the mirror, but that isn't necessarily true if you are married and have children or dependent parents. Every year that you work and pay into the Social Security program, you are also buying protection for your family in the event of your death. Your taxes and earned work credits don't go to waste, even if you die before you retire!

Should you pass away before earning all 40 of your worker credits, you may still meet the requirements needed to provide benefits for your loved ones by achieving either a *fully insured* status or *currently insured* status.

- ***Fully insured*** status means you have earned enough worker credits to give Social Security benefits to your spouse or

39 Center on Budget and Policy Priorities. "Social Security Lifts More People Above the Poverty Line Than Any Other Program." Updated November 9, 2022. Available at https://www.cbpp.org/research/social-security/social-security-lifts-more-people-above-the-poverty-line-than-any-other

former spouse, your surviving and unmarried children and your dependent parents. Fully insured status means your family is entitled to survivor benefits.

- ***Currently insured status***: If you haven't yet earned those 40 worker credits but you have earned at least six work credits in the previous 18 months, then you achieve currently insured status. This status provides survivor benefits to your children and your surviving spouse who is taking care of your children, but it does not provide benefits to your parents or a spouse who is *not* caring for children.

Survivor benefits are similar to life insurance in that they are benefits payable to your family after you die. There are four types of survivor benefits:

1. Payments to your widow or widower and/or your former spouse
2. Payments to your surviving, unmarried children
3. Payments to your dependent parents
4. A one-time lump sum payment to your spouse or children.

There is a limit to the total amount of payments that a family can receive, however. The family maximum payment is the maximum monthly amount that can be paid on one worker's earning record. The formula used to figure that out is very much like the one used to figure out your PIA, but to simplify, it's typically 150–180% of what you're owed at full retirement age.[40]

HOW TO DOUBLE YOUR CHECKS

Most people know about the Social Security payments children can collect if they are disabled or if a parent is disabled or deceased. What most people don't realize, however, is that once you retire and claim

40 Social Security Administration. "Survivors Planner: Maximum Family Amount." Retrieved from SSA.gov.

your retired worker benefit, your unmarried children who are living with you and still going to school can also claim benefits—and you don't have to die first!

This can be a real boost for parents who had children late in life. To qualify, the child must be unmarried and under the age of 18, or under the age of 19 and a full-time student at an elementary or high school.

Fast Fact: The Social Security Administration requires all new beneficiaries to receive their benefit payments via electronic transfer. For children under the age of 18, this means opening a bank account and linking the account and routing number to Social Security.[41]

The child's benefit check will equal half of what you would be entitled to receive at full retirement age, even if you choose to retire early. For example, if you're a 62-year-old mother of a 14-year-old student, you could wait five years until you reach FRA to claim your benefit of $2,000 a month. Alternatively, you could file early while your child is still living with you, receive a reduced check of $1,500, AND get a bonus check for your child amounting to $1,000 a month. That's two checks a month for a total benefit of $2,500.

Of course, the second check will stop coming once the child graduates from high school or turns 19, but you don't have to be stuck with your reduced check. You could choose to voluntarily suspend your benefit. Using our example, you would then receive $2,640 a month once you reach age 70. That's an extra $1,140 a month.

41 U.S. Social Security Administration, "Electronic Payment of Benefits," available at https://www.ssa.gov/deposit/.

Fast Fact: The child benefit for a deceased worker is larger than it is for a retired worker, at 75% of the deceased worker's PIA.[42]

GET THE MOST THAT YOU CAN

In this chapter, we outlined the basic rules and terms so that you could have some understanding of what goes into the calculations when determining claiming strategies. But there's more to it than this. There are even more rules concerning survivor benefits, and most people have far more options available than they realize.

Remember Jane from our story at the beginning of this chapter? She knew she was eligible for a widow's benefit at the age of 60, but she didn't know what that benefit was based on, how much she would get or what her other options were. Because she didn't have a strategy when she filed for her widow's benefit, she also automatically filed for her retirement benefit without knowing. If Jane had restricted her application to widow's benefits only, she could have avoided this outcome and protected her right to claim her own retirement benefit later. That limited her options, and she walked away from an additional $500-plus a month in income without realizing.

Let's take a look at what Jane didn't know:

Note: For simplicity, the following examples do not include cost-of-living adjustments (COLAs). In real life, COLAs would increase the illustrated benefit amounts over time, further magnifying the impact of the chosen strategy.

Option #1: Filing Without a Strategy: In this particular case study, Jane was eligible for a widow's benefit starting at age 60, which would give her $1,430 a month for the rest of her life. If she lives until age 85, then her total lifetime income will be $429,000.

42 Social Security Administration. "Benefits for Children." Retrieved from SSA.gov.

Option #2: A Better Way: Had Jane known about and used a different filing strategy, she could have filed for her widow's benefit at age 60 and received the same $1,430 a month. She could have let her own benefit grow, gaining delayed retirement credits until it reached $1,980 a month at age 70. At that point, if she knows the rules, she could switch to her own benefit. If she lives until age 85, her total lifetime income would be $528,000—an additional $99,000. Best of all, she wouldn't have had to wait or forgo any money early on before starting to receive her checks.

Option #3: Another Better Way: Another strategy Jane could have used involved filing for her own retirement benefit only at age 62, receiving $1,200 a month from ages 62 to 67. Meanwhile, her widow's benefit would grow to its full retirement amount of $2,000. At age 67, she could switch to her widow's benefit and receive $2,000 a month. In this scenario, she wouldn't receive any income from age 60 to 62, which might be desirable if she was still working. If she lives until age 85, her total lifetime income would be $504,000—an additional $75,000.

Understanding the Calculations: How does the Social Security Administration figure all of this out? When calculating benefits for married persons, they use a "simple" Social Security formula that looks like this:

$$B(a) = PIA(a) \times (1 - e(n)) \times (1 + d(n)) \times Z(a) + \max((.5 \times PIA^{*}(a) - PIA(a) \times (1+d(n))) \times E(a), 0) \times (1- u(a,q,n,m)) \times D(a)$$

Should we add: !!??$*@#!!??

No, I'm not making this up, folks. It really does get that complicated. But there's a great deal of money at stake here. Do yourself a favor and make sure you examine your options before you file.

If you've already filed, don't panic. *You might still be eligible for a do-over. You can withdraw your claim within 12 months of filing and refile later to increase your benefits. Keep in mind that you can only do* *this once in your lifetime, and you'll need to repay any benefits you've received so far.*

If you're unsure about your options, consult with a qualified financial advisor with social security optimization training and experience who can help you navigate these complex decisions.

RECAP & WHAT'S NEXT

In this chapter, we continued our journey through Step 2 of the Social Security Path to Clarity™, focusing on the Evaluation phase. We explored the various Social Security claiming options available to married, divorced, and widowed individuals. This chapter highlighted the importance of understanding your options to avoid leaving significant benefits on the table. As illustrated by Jane's story, the decisions you make regarding spousal, divorce, and survivor benefits can have a profound impact on your financial well-being.

To help ensure you're making the most informed decisions, it's essential to evaluate your unique situation thoroughly. The worksheet at the end of this chapter is designed to guide you through this process, helping you identify which benefits you might be eligible for and how to optimize them.

As we move forward, the next chapter will dive deeper into one of the most impactful choices you can make in this Evaluation step—delaying your claim. This decision can potentially increase your monthly benefit, leading to greater financial confidence and security in your retirement years, but it's not right for everyone!

OPTIMIZING SOCIAL SECURITY BENEFITS SELF-ASSESSMENT ™

Making the right decisions about your Social Security benefits can significantly impact your retirement income. This worksheet is designed to help you evaluate your options, understand the rules, and choose the best strategies based on your unique circumstances. Whether you are married, divorced, or widowed, the decisions you make today will affect your financial security for years to come.

DETERMINE IF YOU CAN TAKE ADVANTAGE OF THE FOLLOWING BENEFITS AND RULES:

Spousal Benefits: To qualify for spousal benefits, you must be married for at least one year, the primary worker must be currently receiving benefits, and your benefit based on your own work record must be less than half of the primary worker's PIA.

Will you or do you currently qualify for a spousal benefit?

☐ Yes ☐ No

Will or does your spouse currently qualify for a spousal benefit?

☐ Yes ☐ No

Divorce Benefits: To qualify for divorce benefits, there are two categories to consider:

1. If you have been divorced for less than 2 years, your ex-spouse must be currently receiving Social Security benefits.
2. If you have been divorced for 2 years or longer, you must have been married to your ex-spouse for at least 10 consecutive years, be currently unmarried, and your ex-spouse must be at least age 62. Additionally, you must not qualify for a benefit based on

your own work record that is equal to or greater than half of your ex-spouse's PIA.

Will you or do you currently qualify for a divorce benefit?

☐ Yes ☐ No

Will or does your spouse currently qualify for a divorce benefit?

☐ Yes ☐ No

Survivor Benefits: To qualify for survivor benefits, you must be at least age 60 (or 50 if disabled), and you must not qualify for a benefit based on your own work record that is equal to or greater than the deceased worker's benefit.

Additionally, there are strategic ways to claim survivor benefits to maximize your lifetime income. For example, you could begin collecting the survivor benefit as early as age 60 (or 50 if disabled) and then switch to your own retirement benefit at a later age—such as 70—when it reaches its maximum amount. Alternatively, you may choose to claim your own retirement benefit as early as age 62 and switch to the higher survivor benefit at your full retirement age (FRA).

These strategies depend on your personal circumstances and work history, so it's essential to evaluate which option results in the highest lifetime benefit for you.

Will you or do you currently qualify for a survivor benefit?

☐ Yes ☐ No

Will or does your spouse currently qualify for a survivor benefit?

☐ Yes ☐ No

The Deemed Filing Rule: This was a major change to rules passed by the Bipartisan Budget Act of 2015. It basically says that whenever someone is entitled to receive more than one type of Social Security benefit (such as a divorce benefit and their own benefit) and they file, they are considered to be applying for all available benefits. The SSA will automatically pay you the larger of the two benefit amounts.

IMPORTANTLY, THE DEEMED FILING RULE HAS NEVER APPLIED TO SURVIVOR BENEFITS.

If you are entitled to survivor benefits, you have the flexibility to claim one type of benefit first and then switch to another type later if it results in a larger benefit.

Are you eligible for more than one type of Social Security benefit?

☐ Yes ☐ No

Are you eligible for a survivor benefit?

☐ Yes ☐ No

If you answered yes to both of these questions above, then you may be leaving big bucks on the table. Make an appointment to talk to a financial professional qualified to give Social Security claiming advice.

Social Security Do-Over: You are allowed to withdraw your Social Security application (known as withdrawing your claim) only once, and only if you do it within 12 months of filing for your benefits.

Have you filed for your Social Security benefit?

☐ Yes ☐ No

Date of your filing: ______________________________

Are you eligible for a do-over?

☐ Yes ☐ No

To download a PDF of this worksheet and access additional resources, visit SocialSecurityClarity.com/resources.

CHAPTER 10

THE CASE FOR CLAIMING LATE

Robert was five years older than his spouse, Emily, and everyone they knew was filing early for their Social Security benefit and encouraging the couple to do the same. Robert was 63 and did not know if he should file like his friends or delay the starting age for his benefits

Robert was in good health and still working. They didn't need additional income, and he didn't want to have to reduce his benefits. After coming to one of my Social Security Optimization workshops, it also became clear that he *wanted to make sure that his claiming decision protected his wife.*

Emily was only 58 years of age and both sets of her grandparents had lived into their 90s. Both she and Robert were in good health, and they wanted to retire together. Emily enjoyed her job and wasn't at all ready to retire.

Had Robert listened to the advice of his colleagues and filed earlier at age 63, his benefit would have been $1,800 a month. He would have also had to give back $1 for every $2 he earned to Social Security until he hit his full retirement age if he earned over the annual earnings test amount. The friends telling him that "everyone should file early" were retired or working part-time and not earning enough to exceed the early claiming income threshold.

At age 67, his full retirement benefit was $2,400. But Robert didn't file then either. He retired at age 68 but still waited to file by supplementing their income gap with retirement savings. They worked with their financial planner to get a tax-advantaged plan when pulling out the money from their 401(k), so their filing decision was coordinated with their income plan and the timing of their RMDs.

When Robert turned 70, he filed for his Social Security benefit, which had grown to a substantial $2,976 a month. That gave him $1,176 a month more than he would have gotten had he filed early, but also, it will give his wife more income later in life. Because his benefit check is bigger than hers, when he passes away, she will be entitled to the larger of the two checks.

Working with their adviser, Robert is able to help ensure that Emily will be taken care of even if she lives to be 103. They retired together, and now they can enjoy a future without ever being worried about running out of money.

Robert and Emily represent a minority. According to the Center for Retirement Research at Boston College, only about 6% of men wait until age 70 to claim their Social Security benefits. While many financial planners may advise that we wait until age 70, there are many good reasons to file early. There are also good reasons to file late, most of them financially rewarding, and you may even qualify for filing strategies that can help you earn money while you wait.

The No. 1 reason I hear for filing early is that people want to start getting their money back sooner rather than later because they are afraid the money won't be there. (We addressed the likelihood of that happening in Chapter 8.) I also see people who file early simply because they want to and they don't know any better.

While you may certainly deserve to retire when you are feeling young and spry and ready to travel and do all of the things you've always wanted to do, we certainly don't want you to find out five years later that you're going to run out of money. It is possible to retire early *without* taking your Social Security benefit right away. Most people have far more options than they realize. Here are some important considerations to think about when filing so that you don't look at this decision in isolation and miss out on your better way.

FILLING THE GAPS

Before you decide whether to file now or later, you must first identify your income gaps. Most people have more than one income gap, and the age at which you retire can also create other kinds of gaps. For example, if you retire early at age 62 and you lose your employee health insurance, then you may create a three-year health insurance gap before Medicare kicks in between the ages of 63 and 65.

Fast Fact: You can apply for your Medicare benefits only at the age of 65 and still receive your Social Security retirement benefits later.

An income gap is the difference between what you have and what you need. I have included a worksheet at the end of this chapter so that you can calculate your income gap during retirement. To fill this gap, you may use your retirement savings, investment funds, rental income and benefits from Social Security.

For most people, Social Security represents a major source of income for filling this gap. In fact, around 50% of married Social Security beneficiaries rely on their benefits for 50% or more of their income, while 71% of unmarried beneficiaries depend on Social Security for at least half of their income.[43]

Another important gap to identify is the income loss that will happen after the death of one spouse. While spousal benefits will allow the surviving spouse to keep the higher of the two benefit

43 Social Security Administration, "Fast Facts & Figures About Social Security, 2023." https://www.ssa.gov/news/press/factsheets/basicfact-alt.pdf

checks, the fact is they will be losing one check. Usually, household expenses don't drop drastically just because one spouse passes away.

THE LONG GAME OF RETIREMENT

Your monthly benefit amount can be increased drastically just by delaying the month and the year that you retire. We are living longer and receiving fewer sources of guaranteed income. Social Security is a source of guaranteed income that gives you a regular pay raise in the form of cost-of-living adjustments (COLA) to help offset inflation. Plus, this money is not exposed to stock market risk. Waiting to claim only increases your check—where else can you earn as much as 8% annually without market risk simply by *doing nothing* and waiting to file?

Making the right filing choice about your benefit has become not just important but crucial to the overall success of your retirement. If you don't maximize this opportunity, it could lead to major problems down the road. Before you file, STOP and ask yourself the following three questions:

QUESTION #1: ARE YOU STILL WORKING?

There are limits on how much you can earn while claiming your Social Security benefit. If you earn too much, then you may have to give up some of your benefits. Once you reach the month of your full retirement age, however, there is no limit to how much you can earn.

Working longer can not only put more money into your retirement accounts but it can also increase your monthly Social Security benefit (in addition to the delayed retirement credit). When additional earnings appear on your record, the SSA will check to see whether or not they will increase your monthly benefit.

Remember, they calculate your benefit using your highest-indexed earning years, and it's quite common for people to be in their highest-earning years during the later stages of their career.

That means you can delete those lower-earning years when you were working during high school to get a higher benefit amount!

Fast Fact: If your benefit amount increases based on your additional earnings, the Social Security Administration will send you a letter telling you about your new benefit amount.

QUESTION #2: DOES LONGEVITY RUN IN YOUR FAMILY?

Deciding when to file is a trade-off game: The earlier you file, the earlier you start receiving the benefit checks, but the longer you wait and don't receive checks, the larger the check amount gets. What's the tiebreaker?

Longevity. How long will you live? The longer you live, the more that higher check pays out in your favor, especially when you factor in the cost-of-living adjustments. About one in four 65-year-olds today will live past age 90, and one in 10 will live past age 95.[44] Additionally, nine out of 10 people aged 65 and older are receiving Social Security benefits, and for 32% of them, it represents over 90% of their income.[45]

Fast Fact: Once you file for your benefit, that amount sets the base for the amount that you will receive for the rest of your life.

44 Social Security Administration, "Fact Sheet: Social Security," 2023. Available at https://www.ssa.gov/news/press/factsheets/basicfact-alt.pdf

45 National Institute on Aging, "Longevity and Health," 2022. Available at: https://www.nia.nih.gov/research/dbsr/global-aging

QUESTION #3: DO YOU HAVE OTHER INCOME THAT CAN SUPPORT YOU?

For some people, their Social Security income will not be taxed. For other people, a portion of it may be taxed. If you've been putting money away into a 401(k), 403(b) or any type of retirement account, then you've been saving this money tax-deferred. That means when it comes time to take this money out, you will owe taxes on all of it.

The amount of taxes you'll have to pay is determined by your total income. You may be in the 35% taxable income bracket before retirement and then drop down to the 28% tax bracket after. Or your income tax bracket may stay the same.

It may be beneficial for you to pull out your taxable income early during retirement while letting your Social Security benefit grow, in order to get a more cohesive strategy. Pulling more money from your higher-taxed accounts early on while letting your Social Security benefit grow can mean a lower RMD and lower taxes later on. When combined with an overall withdrawal strategy, it may even increase the longevity of your portfolio.

The Power of Delayed Gratification: A Double Reward

Back in the 1960s, Stanford University Professor Walter Mischel conducted what has now become the famous "marshmallow experiment." He made a deal with young children, promising them two marshmallows if they were able to wait for 15 minutes without eating one marshmallow while he left the room. The experiment became famous because of the humorous antics of the children trying to wait—the squirming, hiding behind their hands, basic agony—all captured on video footage. Perhaps waiting to file for your Social Security benefit makes you feel just the same way.

Or maybe it doesn't.

The most interesting results of the marshmallow experiment came later when follow-up studies found that those children who were able to delay gratification and wait for the double reward were generally smarter, healthier and stronger. They did better in school, had healthier relationships and were more likely to succeed.

If you're someone who has worked hard to save for retirement, then you might be good at delaying gratification. This could also mean you're healthier, stronger and going to live longer. By making the decision to claim later, you just may stand to gain a double helping of lifetime income reward.

RECAP & WHAT'S NEXT

In this chapter, we explored the significant potential financial benefits of delaying your Social Security claim. Delaying your claim can be a powerful strategy, especially for those in good health with longevity in their family. However, it's not a one-size-fits-all solution. The decision to claim early or late should be based on a careful analysis of your unique financial situation.

To help you make this important decision, I've included an **Income Gap Analysis Tool™** at the end of this chapter. This worksheet will guide you through the process of calculating your income gap during retirement and understanding how delaying your Social Security claim can help fill that gap.

As we move forward, the next chapter will discuss the other side of the coin—why some people might choose to file for their Social Security benefits early and how that decision can still be financially sound under certain circumstances.

INCOME GAP ANALYSIS TOOL™

CALCULATE YOUR INCOME GAP

This worksheet is designed to help you evaluate your overall retirement income needs by identifying any income gaps. Use it to calculate how much income you need each month and explore different strategies to fill those gaps. This will set the foundation for more specific planning at the end of the next chapter.

How much income do you need each month?

Amount of income needed per month during retirement: ______

What other sources of guaranteed income do you have? Do you have any pension income? Rental income? Annuity income?

Additional known sources of income per month for yourself:

____

Additional known sources of income for your spouse:______

____

Total sources of household income per month: __________

____

Now calculate your income gap by subtracting the amount needed from the amount of known income. (For example, if you need $6,500 income a month and your total sources of known household income are $2,300, then you would have an income gap of $4,200.)

Your income gap: ______________________________

For a downloadable PDF version of this worksheet, along with additional resources to help you optimize your Social Security strategy, visit SocialSecurityClarity.com/resources

---

CHAPTER 11

GOOD REASONS FOR FILING EARLY

Mike and his wife, Alyssa, decided to file early for their Social Security benefit. Mike was 63 years of age and Alyssa was 62. They both knew that by waiting, they could get more money, but they had other things to consider.

Alyssa was diagnosed with MS at the age of 42. While she wasn't yet in a wheelchair, she knew that she would be someday in the not-too-distant future, and she wanted to travel to Italy while she still could. They had both worked hard for 35 years, and while Mike got a late start on his retirement savings, he'd been making diligent catch-up contributions since the age of 50, and they were in a good financial position.

They worked with a financial adviser who specialized in retirement income planning and income planning. He ran their numbers, and calculated that they were able to comfortably fill their income gap by rolling a portion of their IRAs into income-producing vehicles so that even if the market took a hit, their income would hit the income goal and travel.

Mike and Alyssa felt good about this decision and realized that spending time together and creating memorable experiences was their top priority. *They also were confident after creating a retirement income plan based on their goals* to maximize their remaining active years, *that even if they live to age 100, they will have enough income to enjoy their life.*

Filing early for your benefit locks in a reduced income for life, but it's still an income you can count on, and for many people, this decision is about more than just money. Why do people file early for retirement? Let's take a look at the top three reasons.

TOP 3 REASONS PEOPLE FILE EARLY FOR SOCIAL SECURITY

One of the most common reasons for filing early is health problems. Individuals who are facing significant health challenges often choose to claim their Social Security benefits early, prioritizing immediate financial support over potentially larger future benefits. Mike and Alyssa had time to plan; with other situations, health issues might show up suddenly. This is yet another reason why your savings are so important.

The second most common reason for filing early fell under the umbrella category of "other," and those reasons include wanting to travel, just being ready and because an adviser told them to file. Some individuals prefer to access their benefits earlier to enjoy life experiences while they are still physically capable, even if it means accepting a reduced monthly benefit.

Then there are those people who expected to work until they turned 70, but they find their company is downsizing and they lose their job in their early 60s. This is a time in most people's lives that makes reemployment options difficult to consider. Which brings us to our No. 1 reason:

> ***The most common reason for filing early for Social Security is having to retire earlier than planned.***

For some people, this might come as a welcome surprise. While the full retirement age has gradually increased to 67, many Americans still aim to retire between the ages of 60 and 65, which is often seen as the optimal balance between age and finances. According to the 2024 MassMutual Retirement Happiness Study, 63 is considered the ideal retirement age by both retirees and pre-retirees. While current retirees are hitting close to that mark with an average actual retirement age of 62, there are indications that future retirees could face more challenges in retiring at their ideal age.[46]

These circumstances highlight the importance of being prepared for a potentially longer retirement period than initially planned. With life expectancy increasing, the need for sustainable income over a longer retirement becomes more critical. So, what can you do to prepare?

3 QUESTIONS TO ANSWER BEFORE RETIRING EARLY

The age at which you clock out of the workforce and start relying on the three legs of your stool for income matters, because the earlier you start, the more money you're going to need. If 65% of retired middle-class workers derive more than 50% of their retirement income from Social Security, where is the other 50% going to come from?

That is the question financial professionals like myself have been trying to make people aware of and why I spend so much time teaching people about the importance of financial planning. Over the last four decades, changes to our pension systems across corporate America have put us on the road to a retirement crisis. Based on the latest data, the median retirement account balance for Americans between the ages of 40 and 45 is significantly low relative to what they will need for a comfortable retirement. For example, a 2023 report by Vanguard found that the median 401(k) balance for individuals in this age group is approximately $14,500, which is only a small fraction of the amount experts recommend for retirement savings. Most financial experts suggest that individuals should have a retirement savings of about three times their annual salary by age 40 to be on track for

46 MassMutual Retirement Happiness Study, 2024. Available at: https://www.massmutual.com/global/media/shared/doc/2024_massmutual_retirement_happiness_study.pdf

a secure retirement, highlighting a significant shortfall for many in this age group.[47]

If you are still a few years away from retirement, this is your wake-up call to get aggressive about how you might save. According to a 2022 report by the Employee Benefit Research Institute (EBRI), approximately 47% of retirees left the workforce earlier than planned, often due to factors such as health issues, disability, or changes at their company. This underscores the importance of preparing for the possibility of an early retirement, even if it isn't part of the initial plan.[48]

Before you decide to retire early, STOP and make sure you're prepared to face the realities.

QUESTION #1: WHAT WILL YOU DO FOR HEALTH INSURANCE?

Many American workers lose more than just their paycheck when they retire; they often lose their employer-provided health insurance benefits, too. Since Medicare eligibility generally begins at age 65, those who retire earlier need to find alternative health coverage until they reach that age. Here are five strategies to consider:

1. **Spouse's Health Insurance**: If you are married and your spouse is still working, you may be able to switch to your spouse's employer-sponsored health insurance plan. This can be a cost-effective way to maintain coverage until you become eligible for Medicare.

2. **COBRA Coverage**: You may temporarily extend your employer-provided health insurance through COBRA (Consolidated Omnibus Budget Reconciliation Act) benefits. COBRA allows you to keep your existing health insurance for up to 18 months

---

47 Vanguard. "How America Saves 2023: An In-Depth Look at the Savings Behavior of 5 Million Retirement Plan Participants." 2023.

48 Employee Benefit Research Institute (EBRI), 2022 Retirement Confidence Survey, available at ebri.org

(and in some cases longer), but you'll need to pay the full premium, which can be expensive.

3. **Retiree Medical Insurance**: Check whether you're eligible for retiree medical insurance through your employer or your spouse's employer. This option is increasingly rare, but it's worth investigating if available.

4. **Marketplace Coverage**: You can purchase health insurance through the Health Insurance Marketplace established under the Affordable Care Act (ACA). The Marketplace offers a variety of plans, and depending on your income, you might qualify for subsidies to lower your premiums. Pre-existing conditions cannot disqualify you from coverage.

5. **State-Sponsored Programs**: Some states offer their own health insurance programs that may be available to retirees under certain circumstances. While universal health care is not widely available, some states have expanded Medicaid or offer other forms of public health insurance for those who qualify.

Fast Facts: You may qualify for COBRA continued group health benefits provided by your group health insurance plan under the following circumstances:

- *Voluntary or involuntary job loss*
- *Reduction in the hours worked*
- *Transition between jobs*
- *Death of the employee*
- *Divorce or legal separation*
- *Other life events such as retirement*

QUESTION #2: HOW IS YOUR HEALTH?

And speaking of health insurance, how have you been feeling lately? In my first book, *The RichLife: 10 Investment for True Wealth*, a lot of my readers were surprised to see an entire chapter devoted to your primary asset: YOU.

In my practice, I sometimes see people who are so focused on earning money, they forget to take care of themselves. This can cost you dearly during retirement. Indeed, studies find that changes in retirement expectations and happiness have more to do with an abundance of health than an abundance of wealth. But if you retire early, will you feel better?

POSITIVE HEALTH OUTCOMES ASSOCIATED WITH EARLY RETIREMENT:

Recent research indicates that early retirement can have positive effects on health outcomes, particularly when individuals engage in fulfilling activities, maintain strong social connections, and manage stress effectively. The transition to retirement, when managed well, can lead to improved physical and mental health, as retirees have more time for exercise, hobbies, and spending time with loved ones, all of which contribute to overall well-being.[49]

CHALLENGES AND RISKS ASSOCIATED WITH RETIREMENT:

On the other hand, retirement can present challenges for some individuals. Retirement can sometimes lead to feelings of isolation, loss of identity, and depression, particularly for those who lack a strong social network or purpose post-retirement. The loss of routine

49 HelpGuide. "Adjusting to Retirement: Handling the Challenges and Opportunities." https://www.helpguide.org/aging/healthy-aging/adjusting-to-retirement

and social connections from the workplace may contribute to these negative feelings, highlighting the importance of staying active and engaged in meaningful activities after retiring.[50]

The evidence seems to suggest that it's not just the act of retiring that can lead to greater happiness, but being purposeful about the kinds of things you'll be doing during retirement. If you focus on those things that money can't buy, such as meaningful experiences and time with loved ones, then retiring at a reduced income might give you a greater sense of fulfillment. It's not just about the money.

Fast Fact: Recent guidelines from the U.S. Department of Health and Human Services recommend that adults engage in at least 150 minutes of moderate-intensity aerobic physical activity, such as brisk walking, or 75 minutes of vigorous-intensity activity, such as running, each week. This activity can help reduce symptoms of depression and anxiety, improving overall mental health and well-being.[51]

QUESTION #3: DO YOU HAVE OTHER INCOME TO SUPPORT YOU?

Filing for Social Security early can have significant implications, particularly when it comes to your ability to work and earn additional income. If you file before reaching your Full Retirement Age (FRA) and continue to work, your benefits may be temporarily reduced based on your earnings.

- **If you are under FRA**, Social Security will deduct $1 from your benefits for every $2 you earn above the annual limit.

50 Ibid

51 U.S. Department of Health and Human Services. "Physical Activity Guidelines for Americans, 2nd edition." Health.gov.

- **In the year you reach FRA**, a different earnings test applies. For the months leading up to your FRA, Social Security will deduct $1 for every $3 you earn above a higher annual limit.

Once you reach FRA, the earnings limit no longer applies, and your benefits are recalculated to give you credit for the months that benefits were reduced.

Moreover, filing early could reduce the survivor benefits your spouse might receive later. Since survivor benefits are based on the benefit amount the deceased spouse was receiving (or was eligible to receive) at the time of death, filing early can result in a permanently reduced benefit for your surviving spouse.

Although certain Social Security strategies, such as "File and Suspend" and "Restricted Application," have been eliminated for all individuals, there may still be ways to optimize your benefits based on your situation. It's crucial to consider all factors, including other sources of income and how they interact with your Social Security benefits.

WEIGHING THE PROS AND THE CONS

Your Social Security claiming decision is one that will go on to affect the rest of your life, and if you are married, then it will also affect the life of your spouse. It deserves your focused attention. Once you file, that income amount becomes the base from which all your future COLAs are calculated. If you file early and take a 30% reduction in your full retirement amount, you do not get that full retirement amount once you reach full retirement age. That 30% reduction is for life.

On the other hand, when you file early, you receive a few extra years of income when you are young and ready to enjoy it. Claiming at the reduced amount may reduce your total income for life, but if you employ a strategy, it might also be possible for a couple to work together and retire with health, wealth and a sense of fulfillment.

RECAP AND WHAT'S NEXT

In this chapter, we explored the good reasons for filing early for Social Security benefits. Whether it's due to health issues, an unexpected job loss, or simply wanting to enjoy life sooner, many people find that filing early makes the most sense for their circumstances. Before making your decision, it's essential to weigh the pros and cons and consider your unique situation.

As we conclude Step 2: Evaluation, you now have a clearer picture of how different claiming strategies can impact your retirement. In the final section, Part 3: Implementation, we'll dive into how to put these strategies into action!

Before moving forward, take a moment to complete the worksheet at the end of this chapter. This exercise will help you calculate your options for filling any income gaps in your retirement plan, setting the stage for a smooth transition into the implementation phase.

INCOME GAP FUNDING WORKSHEET™

CALCULATE YOUR OPTIONS FOR FILLING YOUR INCOME GAP

This worksheet is a continuation of the income gap analysis from Chapter 10. Here, you'll take a closer look at how your Social Security benefits, combined with other income strategies, can fill those gaps. Be sure to reference your calculations from the previous chapter to get a complete picture of your retirement income plan.

What is your income gap? (From Chapter 10): ________________

How much of your income gap can Social Security fill?

How much income will you receive per month at age 62?

For yourself: ___________For your spouse: _________________

How much Social Security income will you receive per month at FRA?

For yourself: ___________For your spouse: _________________

How much Social Security income will you receive per month at age 70?

For yourself: ___________For your spouse: _________________

What sources of non guaranteed income do you have?

Total assets that are tax-qualified (IRA, 401(k), etc.): __________
Total assets that are nonqualified (Roth IRA, IUL, etc.): _______

What income-producing options are you most familiar with? *(Check all that apply.)*

- ☐ The 4% withdrawal rule using market investments
- ☐ Payments from stock dividends
- ☐ Payments from bonds
- ☐ Immediate annuities

- ☐ Fixed-indexed annuities with income riders*
- ☐ Variable annuities*
- ☐ Fixed annuities*

By completing this worksheet, you've taken a significant step toward identifying the potential sources to fund your retirement income gap.

Use this worksheet as a guide to discuss your options with your financial advisor and to develop a comprehensive strategy that aligns with your retirement goals. Whether you decide to draw from investment accounts, consider annuities, or explore other income-producing strategies, this worksheet provides the foundation for making informed decisions.

For a downloadable PDF version of this INCOME GAP FUNDING WORKSHEET™ and additional resources to help you further refine your retirement strategy, visit SocialSecurityClarity.com/resources.

Disclaimer: *Fixed Annuities are long term insurance contracts and there is a surrender charge imposed generally during the first 5 to 7 years that you own the annuity contract. Indexed annuities are insurance contracts that depending on the contract may offer a guaranteed annual interest rate and some participation growth, if any, of a stock market index. Such contracts have substantial variation in terms, costs of guarantees and features and may cap participation or returns in significant ways. Investors are cautioned to carefully review an indexed annuity for its features, costs, risks, and how the variables are calculated. Any guarantees offered are backed by the financial strength of the insurance company. Surrender charges apply if not held to the end of the term. Withdrawals are taxed as ordinary income and, if taken prior to 59 1/2, a 10% federal tax penalty.

Please consider the investment objectives, risks, charges and expenses carefully before investing in Variable Annuities. The prospectus, which contains this and other information about the variable annuity contract and the underlying investment options, can be obtained from the insurance company or your financial professional. Be sure to read the prospectus carefully before deciding whether to invest.

The investment return and principal value of the variable annuity investment options are not guaranteed. Variable annuity sub-accounts fluctuate with changes in market conditions. The principal may be worth more or less than the original amount invested when the annuity is surrendered.

PART 3

IMPLEMENTATION

Congratulations on reaching the final stage of our journey—Implementation. Now that you've carefully evaluated your Social Security options and developed a strategy that aligns with your retirement goals, it's time to take action.

Implementation is all about making sure your chosen strategy is executed smoothly and effectively. In this section, you'll find practical guidance, to help ensure every step of your plan is covered.

WHAT TO EXPECT:

- **Master Checklist:** Summaries of essential steps highlighted at the end of each chapter to reinforce your understanding and readiness.
- **Social Security FAQ:** An at-a-glance resource of top questions and answers.

For a comprehensive overview, the full Social Security Clarity Master Checklist™ is available as a downloadable PDF at SocialSecurityClarity.com/resources. This resource recaps the entire 3-step process—Preparation, Evaluation, and Implementation—with key action items and resources gathered throughout this book.

The goal of Part 3: Implementation is to ensure you have everything in place to successfully activate your Social Security strategy. With this final phase, you can move forward confidently with your decisions.

As always, it's best to consult with a knowledgeable advisor who can tailor advice to your unique situation. Use the guidance in this section as a conversation starter with your advisor to ensure your Social Security strategy is both personalized and optimized.

Let's dive in and turn your strategy into action!

CHAPTER 12

THE SOCIAL SECURITY CLARITY MASTER CHECKLIST™

"What you do today can improve all your tomorrows."
— RALPH MARSTON

Welcome to the final step in your Social Security journey—**The Social Security Success Master Checklist™**. This chapter serves as a gateway to all the worksheets and actionable steps you've encountered throughout the book as a downloadable PDF, providing you with easy access to this comprehensive guide, helping ensure you're fully prepared to make the best decisions for your Social Security benefits. Whether you've already started filling out the worksheets in the book or are just getting started, this comprehensive checklist will serve as your go-to resource for aligning your retirement strategy with your personal goals.

AVAILABLE WORKSHEETS:

- Social Security Tax Strategy Guide™
- Spousal Social Security Checklist™
- Earnings Impact Calculator™
- Claiming Strategy Evaluation Worksheet™
- Social Security Fraud Defense Checklist™
- Future Income Assessment Worksheet™
- Household Benefits Optimizer™
- Optimizing Social Security Benefits Self Assessment™
- Income Gap Analysis Tool™
- Income Gap Funding Worksheet™

The Social Security Success Master Checklist™ consolidates all the key actions and decisions you've explored in previous chapters, from calculating your income gap to choosing the optimal time to file for your benefits. It's designed to be a practical tool that you can revisit as needed, helping you stay on track and make informed choices as you approach retirement.

As you complete this final step, it's crucial to revisit the three-step process outlined in this book: **Preparation, Evaluation, and Implementation**. Each step has provided you with the tools and knowledge to make informed decisions about your Social Security benefits. However, the journey doesn't end here.

Meeting with a knowledgeable financial advisor is the best way to review your answers and help ensure that your strategy is tailored to your specific needs and goals. An advisor can help you navigate any complexities and fine-tune your plan for optimal results.

To assist you further, all the worksheets included in this Master Checklist can be downloaded as a PDF from SocialSecurityClarity.com/resources, along with additional tools and resources to support your Social Security decisions.

CHAPTER 13

SOCIAL SECURITY FAQS

"Knowledge is power."
– SIR FRANCIS BACON

Use this chapter as a quick reference guide with basic information about claiming your retirement benefit including delayed retirement credits, spousal benefit qualifications, earning thresholds, etc.

All Social Security-related data and guidelines in this chapter are based on information provided by the Social Security Administration as of 2024. For more detailed information, visit www.ssa.gov.

TERMS AND ACRONYMS:

FRA is your full retirement age. This is the age at which you become entitled to your full or unreduced retirement benefits.

Broadly speaking:

- For people born before 1937, the FRA is 65.
- For people born between the years 1943 and 1954, FRA is 66.

- For people born in 1960 or later, FRA is 67.

PIA is the primary insurance amount is the amount your benefit will be if you file at your full retirement age. When you file at your FRA, your benefit is neither reduced for early retirement nor increased for delayed retirement.

SSA is the Social Security Administration.

WHO QUALIFIES FOR SOCIAL SECURITY?

- **40 Credits Requirement:** To qualify for retirement benefits, you need to earn 40 credits over your lifetime. These credits are based on your earnings. In 2025, you earn one credit for each **$1,810** in earnings, and you can earn up to four credits per year. This means that earning at least $7,240 in a year will give you the maximum four credits.
- **Spousal Benefits:** Even if you haven't worked under the Social Security system, you might still qualify for **spousal benefits** and **Medicare** at age 65, even without earning 40 work credits, if you meet the following criteria:
    - You are at least **62 years of age**.
    - You are **married**.
    - Your spouse is currently receiving retirement or disability benefits.
- **Divorced Spouse Benefits:** If you are divorced, you may qualify for divorced spouse benefits in one of two scenarios. In either case, you may qualify for a divorced spouse benefit equal to up to 50% of your ex-spouse's full retirement age benefit amount, provided your own Social Security benefit is less than half of theirs.

1. **Divorced for Less Than 2 Years**
    - Your ex-spouse must be **currently receiving** Social Security retirement or disability benefits.

- You must be **at least age 62.**
- Your marriage lasted **at least 10 consecutive years.**

2. **Divorced for 2 Years or Longer**
    - You and your ex-spouse must both be **at least age 62.**
    - Your marriage lasted **at least 10 consecutive years.**
    - **You are currently unmarried.**

- **Survivor Benefits:**

If you are a survivor, you may choose to receive the larger of:

- Your own benefit check.
- The benefit check of the deceased.
- Or, you can choose to start with one benefit and switch to the other later, allowing the benefit you delay to grow.

- **Eligibility for Survivor Benefits:**
    - Survivor benefits generally require that you be at least **60 years old** (or **50** if disabled). If you remarry before age 60, you will lose eligibility for survivor benefits. However, if you remarry after age 60, you can still collect survivor benefits based on your deceased spouse's record.

WHEN DO YOU GET PAID?

- **If your birthday falls between the 1st and the 10th of the month:** You will receive your check on the **second Wednesday** of the month.
- **If your birthday falls between the 11th and the 20th of the month:** You will receive your check on the **third Wednesday** of the month.
- **If your birthday falls between the 21st and the end of the month:** You will receive your check on the **fourth Wednesday** of the month.

WHAT ARE THE PENALTIES FOR FILING EARLY?

If you claim Social Security benefits before your Full Retirement Age (FRA), your benefit will be permanently reduced based on how many months early you start receiving benefits. This reduction is often referred to as an actuarial reduction. Here's how it works:

- If you start benefits at **age 62**, the earliest age at which you can claim, your benefit is reduced by approximately **25%** (for those with an FRA of 66). This means you would receive **75%** of what your benefit would be if you had waited until your FRA.
- The reduction is less severe for each year you delay claiming between ages 62 and 66. For someone with a Primary Insurance Amount (PIA) of $1,000 and an FRA of 66, the reduction would look like this:
    - **Age 62:** $750 (75% of the PIA)
    - **Age 63:** $800 (80% of the PIA)
    - **Age 64:** $867 (86.7% of the PIA)
    - **Age 65:** $933 (93.3% of the PIA)
        - **For those born after 1954,** the FRA is gradually increasing from 66 to 67. If your FRA is 67, claiming at 62 results in approximately a **30%** reduction. This means that at age 62, you would receive about **70%** of your PIA, rather than 75%.
        - The reduction percentages depend on your specific FRA, so it's important to consult the Social Security Administration (SSA) or a financial advisor to get precise figures based on your birth year.

WHAT ARE THE REWARDS FOR WAITING TO FILE?

If you claim Social Security benefits after your Full Retirement Age (FRA), the Social Security Administration (SSA) rewards you with Delayed Retirement Credits (DRCs). These credits increase your benefit by a certain percentage for each year you delay claiming beyond your FRA, up until age 70. The percentage increase varies based on your birth year.

- For those with a Full Retirement Age of 67, delaying benefits can increase your monthly benefit by **8% per year**.

For someone with a Primary Insurance Amount (PIA) of $1,000 and an FRA of 67, the rewards for waiting to file might look like this:

- **Age 68:** $1,080 (an 8% increase)
- **Age 69:** $1,160 (a 16% increase)
- **Age 70:** $1,240 (a 24% increase)

This increase is particularly valuable as it permanently boosts the monthly benefit amount, providing a higher income throughout retirement. It's important to note that these credits stop accumulating after age 70, so there's no benefit to delaying beyond that age.

WHAT ARE THE RULES FOR SPOUSAL BENEFITS?

Spousal benefits were designed to protect the individual who worked in partnership taking care of the home and raising children. They may be eligible to receive up to 50% of their spouses PIA. To qualify for spousal benefits, you must meet the following criteria:

✓ Have been married at least one year.

✓ Have a spouse who has already filed for their benefit.

✓ Have a PIA benefit that is less than one-half the PIA of your spouse.

Early Filing Penalty: If you file for spousal benefits before reaching your FRA, the benefit will be reduced. The reduction is permanent and depends on how early you start receiving the benefit.

Deemed Filing: If you were born on or after January 2, 1954, when you file for either your retirement benefits or spousal benefits, you are "deemed" to be filing for both, and you will receive the higher of the two amounts.

Maximum Benefit: The 50% spousal benefit is the maximum you can receive and only applies if you wait until your FRA to begin benefits. If you take benefits earlier, they will be reduced.

WHAT ARE THE RULES FOR DIVORCE BENEFITS?

Divorce benefits apply to both ex-spouses, including those in same-sex marriages, provided certain criteria are met. If you qualify, you can receive a benefit equal to 50% of your ex-spouse's Primary Insurance Amount (PIA) at your Full Retirement Age (FRA). If your own benefit based on your work record is higher than 50% of your ex-spouse's PIA, you will receive your own benefit instead.

Facts about divorce benefits:

- **Your ex-spouse's influence**: Your ex-spouse has no say in whether or not you can file for divorce benefits, and your claiming benefits will not reduce or affect the payout your ex-spouse receives.
- **Confidentiality**: Your ex-spouse will not be notified when you apply for or receive benefits based on their work record.

Eligibility Criteria:

- **Marital status**: You must be currently unmarried to claim benefits based on your ex-spouse's work record.
- **Marriage duration**: You and your ex-spouse must have been married for at least 10 consecutive years.
- **Age**: Both you and your ex-spouse must be at least age 62.
- **Timing after divorce**: You and your ex-spouse must have been divorced for at least two years, or your ex must already be receiving Social Security retirement or disability benefits.

- **Remarriage**: If you remarry, you typically cannot collect benefits on your former spouse's record unless your subsequent marriage ends (whether by death, divorce, or annulment).
- **Eligibility for Spousal Benefits**: If your ex-spouse has not applied for benefits but is eligible for them, you can still receive benefits if you have been divorced for at least two years and both of you are at least age 62.
- **Deemed Filing**: If you were born on or after January 2, 1954, you will be "deemed" to be filing for both your own benefits and any benefits you are eligible for based on your ex-spouse's record when you apply. You will receive the higher of the two amounts.

WHAT ARE THE RULES FOR SURVIVOR BENEFITS?

When your spouse passes away, the household will lose one Social Security benefit check. Survivor benefits, also known as widow or widower benefits, are designed to provide financial support to the surviving spouse. As the survivor, you have two main options:

- **Receive your own benefit check** based on your own work record.
- **Receive the benefit check of your deceased spouse**, if it is larger than your own benefit.

Additionally, you can choose to switch between benefits at different times to maximize your total income. For example:

- You could begin collecting survivor benefits as early as age 60 and later switch to your own retirement benefit at age 70, when it reaches its maximum.
- Alternatively, you could collect your own benefit as early as age 62 and switch to the survivor benefit at your full retirement age (FRA) if it is larger.

It's important to note that the Social Security Administration will determine which benefit provides the higher amount and guide you through the process.

Eligibility Criteria:

- **Age Requirement**: You must be a widow or widower at least 60 years old (or 50 if disabled) to qualify for survivor benefits.
- **Marital Status**: You must be unmarried unless you remarry after age 60 (or after age 50 if disabled). Remarrying before this age generally disqualifies you from receiving survivor benefits, though there are exceptions.
- **Duration of Marriage**: You must have been married to the deceased for at least nine months prior to their death, although exceptions exist, such as in cases of accidental death.

Important Facts about Survivor Benefits:

- **Survivor benefits have never been subject to the deeming rule**: This means you are not automatically deemed to be applying for all benefits for which you are eligible, allowing more flexibility in choosing the best benefit option.
- **Multiple Benefit Eligibility**: If you are eligible for more than one type of benefit (e.g., your own retirement benefit and survivor benefits), you may be able to employ a filing strategy that allows one benefit to grow while receiving the other.
- **Maximizing Benefits**: If you choose to delay your retirement benefit while receiving survivor benefits, your retirement benefit can continue to grow due to delayed retirement credits, allowing you to switch to a higher benefit amount later.
- **Timing of Benefit Receipt**: If you are already receiving Social Security benefits on your own record and your spouse passes away, you can switch to the higher survivor benefit.
- **Benefit Reduction**: If you claim survivor benefits before reaching your full retirement age (FRA), the benefit amount will be reduced, similar to early retirement benefits. However,

if you wait until FRA or later, you can receive 100% of your deceased spouse's benefit.

- **Impact of Delayed Filing by Deceased**: If your spouse delayed claiming their benefits past their FRA, the survivor benefits you receive could be higher than the deceased's PIA due to delayed retirement credits.

WHAT FILING STRATEGIES ARE AVAILABLE FOR CLAIMING SOCIAL SECURITY?

- **Delaying Benefits for Higher Payments**: If you are married, allowing the higher earner's benefit to grow by delaying filing can provide additional income for the surviving spouse. Delayed retirement credits increase the benefit amount by up to 8% per year beyond your full retirement age (FRA) up until age 70.
- **Survivor Benefits Strategy**: If you are a widow or widower, you may be eligible to file for survivor benefits while allowing your retirement benefits to grow, or vice versa. This strategy allows for flexibility in maximizing the total benefits received over a lifetime.
- **Withdrawing Your Application**: If you filed for Social Security benefits and later decide that you would like to change your filing decision, you have the option to withdraw your application within 12 months of filing. However, you must repay any benefits received to take advantage of this option. Note that this withdrawal option is only available once in your lifetime.
- **File and Suspend**: The "file and suspend" strategy was eliminated by the Bipartisan Budget Act of 2015. As of April 30, 2016, you can no longer file for benefits and suspend them to earn delayed retirement credits while allowing your spouse to claim spousal benefits. Therefore, this strategy **is no longer available.**

WHAT ARE THE PENALTIES FOR WORKING WHILE CLAIMING SOCIAL SECURITY?

You can work while receiving your Social Security retirement benefits, but whether your benefit is reduced depends on two factors:

1. **Your Earnings**: How much money you earn from work.
2. **Your Full Retirement Age (FRA)**: The age at which you are entitled to your full Social Security benefit without reductions.

- **If you are under your full retirement age and working**: The Social Security Administration (SSA) will deduct $1 from your benefits for every $2 you earn above the annual earnings limit. For 2025, the annual earnings limit is **$23,400**. This limit typically increases each year, so it's important to check the current limit for the year you are filing.
- **If you reach full retirement age during the year**: SSA will deduct $1 from your benefits for every $3 you earn above a higher earnings limit, which applies only to earnings before the month you reach FRA. For 2025, the annual earnings limit for this situation is **$62,160**. The same adjustment applies for subsequent years as the limit is adjusted annually.
- **If you are past your full retirement age and working**: The SSA will no longer reduce your benefits, regardless of how much you earn, starting with the month you reach FRA. At this point, your benefits are recalculated to credit you for any months in which your benefits were reduced due to excess earnings.

Key Notes:

- The earnings limit applies only to income from work (wages or self-employment income). It does not include investment income, pensions, annuities, or other non-work sources.
- If your benefits are reduced due to excess earnings, the SSA will increase your benefit amount starting at your full retirement

age to account for the months in which your benefits were withheld.

Ensure you verify the annual earnings limits with the SSA or a financial advisor for the most accurate and up-to-date information.

WHAT ARE THE PROVISIONAL INCOME TAX THRESHOLDS FOR SOCIAL SECURITY?

As of 2025, the provisional income tax thresholds that determine how much of your Social Security benefits may be subject to federal income tax are as follows:

- **If you file a federal tax return as an "individual" and your provisional income is**:
- **Less than $25,000**: You may not have to pay any federal income taxes on your Social Security benefits.
- **Between $25,000 and $34,000**: You may have to pay income tax on up to 50% of your benefits.
- **More than $34,000**: Up to 85% of your benefits may be taxable.
- **If you file a joint return** (married filing jointly):
- **Less than $32,000**: You may not have to pay any federal income taxes on your Social Security benefits.
- **Between $32,000 and $44,000**: You may have to pay income tax on up to 50% of your benefits.
- **More than $44,000**: Up to 85% of your benefits may be taxable.
- **If you are married and file a separate tax return**:
- You will likely pay taxes on your Social Security benefits, regardless of your income level.

Additional Notes:

- **Combined Income**: For Social Security tax purposes, combined income is calculated as your adjusted gross income (AGI) before Social Security benefits, plus non-taxable interest, plus half of your Social Security benefits.

- **Threshold Stability:** The thresholds for taxation have remained largely unchanged for many years and do not adjust for inflation, which means more people may be subject to taxes on their Social Security benefits over time.

ACTION ITEMS:

- **Consultation:** It's advisable to consult with a tax professional or financial advisor to understand how your Social Security benefits might be taxed based on your specific situation and to discuss potential strategies for minimizing taxes on your benefits.

HOW DO YOU FILE FOR YOUR SOCIAL SECURITY?

You may file for your Social Security benefits in one of the following three ways:

1. **Online:** You can file for your benefits through the official Social Security website by visiting www.ssa.gov.
2. **Phone:** Call the Social Security Administration at 1-800-772-1213. If you have a hearing impairment, you can use the TTY number at 1-800-325-0778.
3. **In Person:** Visit your local Social Security office. While an appointment is not required, calling ahead to schedule one can reduce the time you spend waiting.

WHEN SHOULD YOU FILE FOR YOUR SOCIAL SECURITY?

It is generally recommended to apply for Social Security benefits approximately 90 days before your desired start date. This timing ensures that you have enough time to complete the application process and avoid any delays in receiving your benefits.

For more resources on your biggest Social Security questions and to submit your mailbag questions for a chance of being answered on *The RichLife Retirement Show*, visit SocialSecurityClarity.com/resources.

CHAPTER 14

PUTTING YOUR PLAN INTO ACTION

"Action is the foundational key to all success."
– PABLO PICASSO

You've now completed a comprehensive journey through the intricate world of Social Security Clarity, armed with the knowledge and tools to make informed decisions that will impact your retirement. From the groundwork of preparation to the critical evaluations and finally to the implementation of your strategy, you are now equipped to navigate this crucial aspect of your financial future with confidence.

But remember, the true power of knowledge lies in action. As you close this book, take a moment to reflect on the steps you've learned and commit to taking the next action. Whether it's filling out the worksheets, revisiting your strategy, or scheduling a meeting with your financial advisor, the steps you take today will shape the security and comfort of your tomorrow.

Your Social Security benefits are not just a government program—they are a cornerstone of your retirement. By applying the strategies you've learned, you are taking control of your financial future, helping ensure that you maximize the benefits you've earned.

To continue your journey, revisit the **Social Security Clarity Master Checklist™** whenever needed and consult with a knowledgeable financial advisor to tailor your plan to your unique needs. Remember, my team and I are here as a resource to guide you through this process. For all the tools and resources mentioned in this book, as well as to sign up for continued updates on important changes to Social Security including free lifetime updates to this book, visit SocialSecurityClarity.com/resources.

Made in United States
North Haven, CT
10 November 2026

22106114R00098